QUEEN MARY 2

*The Greatest Ocean Liner
of Our Time*

QUEEN

MARY 2

The Greatest Ocean Liner of Our Time

John Maxtone-Graham

photographs by Harvey Lloyd

with contributions from Michel Verdure and Yves Guillotin

Bulfinch Press
New York • Boston • London

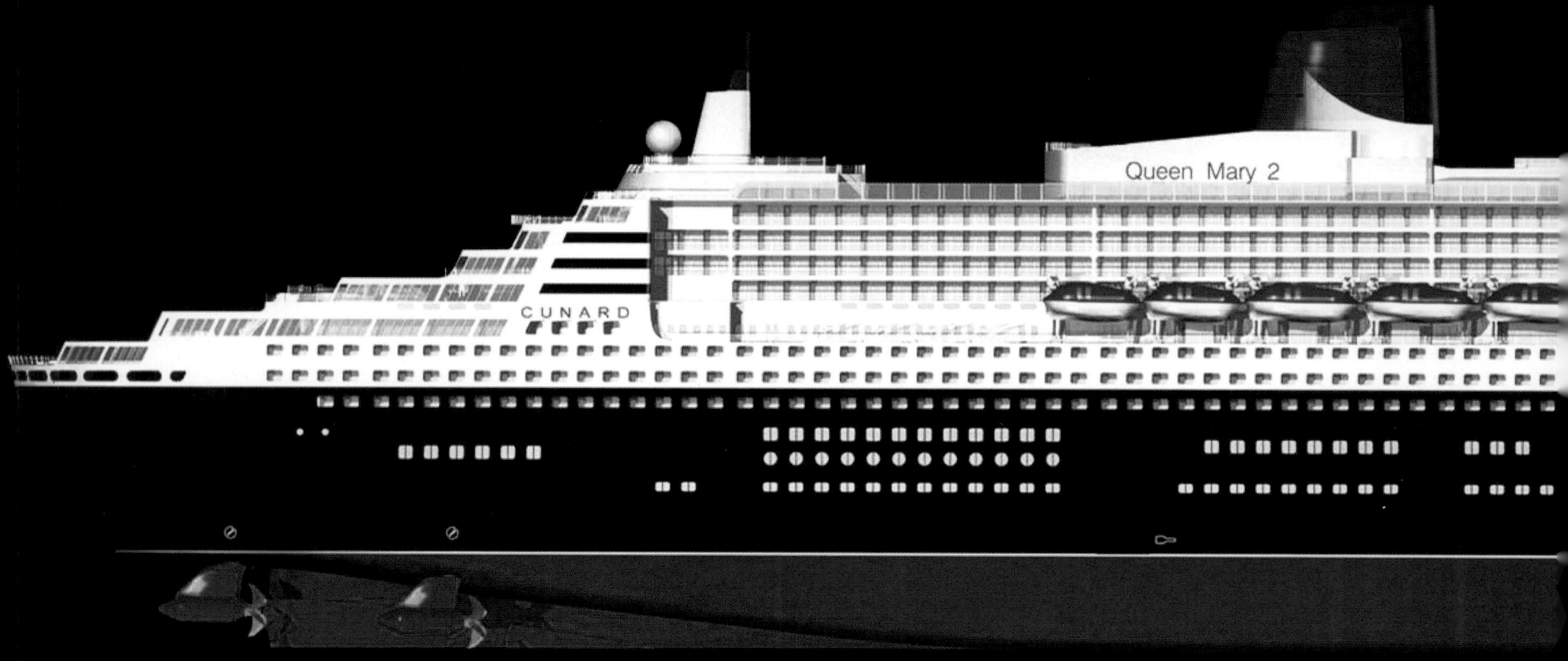
Queen Mary 2
CUNARD

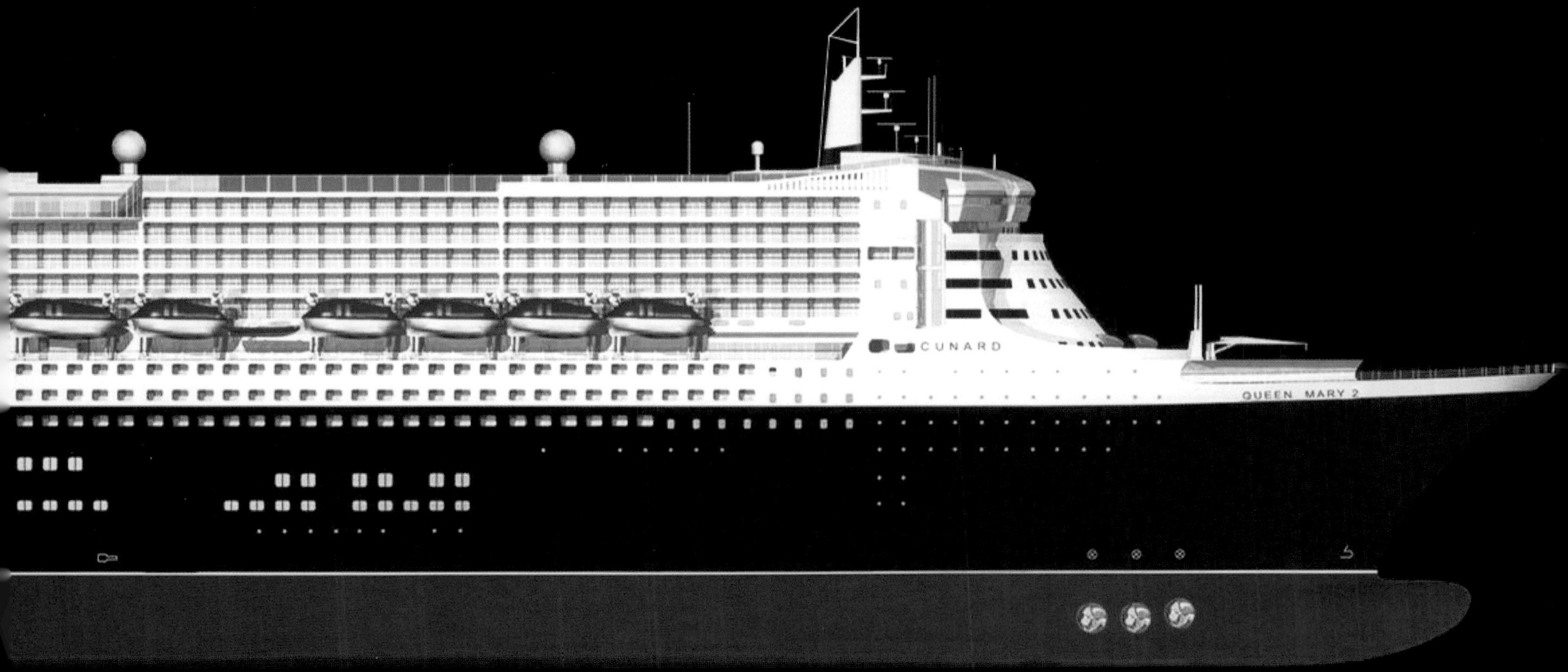
CUNARD
QUEEN MARY 2

Text © 2004 by John Maxtone-Graham
Chairman's Foreword © 2004 Micky Arison
Commodore's Foreword © 2004 Commodore Ron W. Warwick
Cunarder's Chart © 2004 John Maxtone-Graham
"Photographing an Icon" © 2004 Harvey Lloyd
Photographs copyright © 2004 per list on page 204

Bulfinch Press
Hachette Book Group
237 Park Avenue, New York, NY 10017
Visit our Web site at www.HachetteBookGroup.com

Produced by Carpe Diem Books

First Edition
Second Printing, 2008

Bulfinch is an imprint of Little, Brown and Company. The Bulfinch name and logo are
trademarks of Hachette Book Group, Inc.

ISBN 978-0-8212-2884-5
Library of Congress Control Number 2003116444

Book design by Reynolds/Wulf Design, Inc.

Printed in China

Opposite: The rampant lion became the company symbol when
Cunard went public in 1878. Irreverent wags along Liverpool's
waterfront christened it "the monkey wi' the nut." *Page 8–9: Queen
Mary 2's* construction starts early on a foggy morning in Forme B.
Page 10–11: Invited travel press representatives pose in a grand-
stand beneath *Queen Mary 2's* completed bow in March 2003.
Page 12–13: Under way at sea for the first time, *Queen Mary 2* cuts
a fine maritime figure in late September 2003. *Page 15:* One of the
vessel's four revolutionary Mermaid pods, complete with burnished,
stainless steel propeller, comes in for a landing before installation.

Contents

Forewords 17

Preface 18

The Giant in Prospect 20

Cunard Enrichment 48

Sir Samuel's Novel Service 90

King of the Atlantic 94

Nineteenth Century Cunard Shipboard 98

Teutonic Challenge, Cunard Response 102

Three Predecessor *Queens* 112

Twentieth Century Cunard Shipboard 120

Hull #G32 126

Queen Mary 2 Emerges 144

Finale & Debut 174

Twenty-first Century Cunard Shipboard 190

Bibliography 202

Photographing an Icon 203

Acknowledgments 203

Photo Credits 204

Index 205

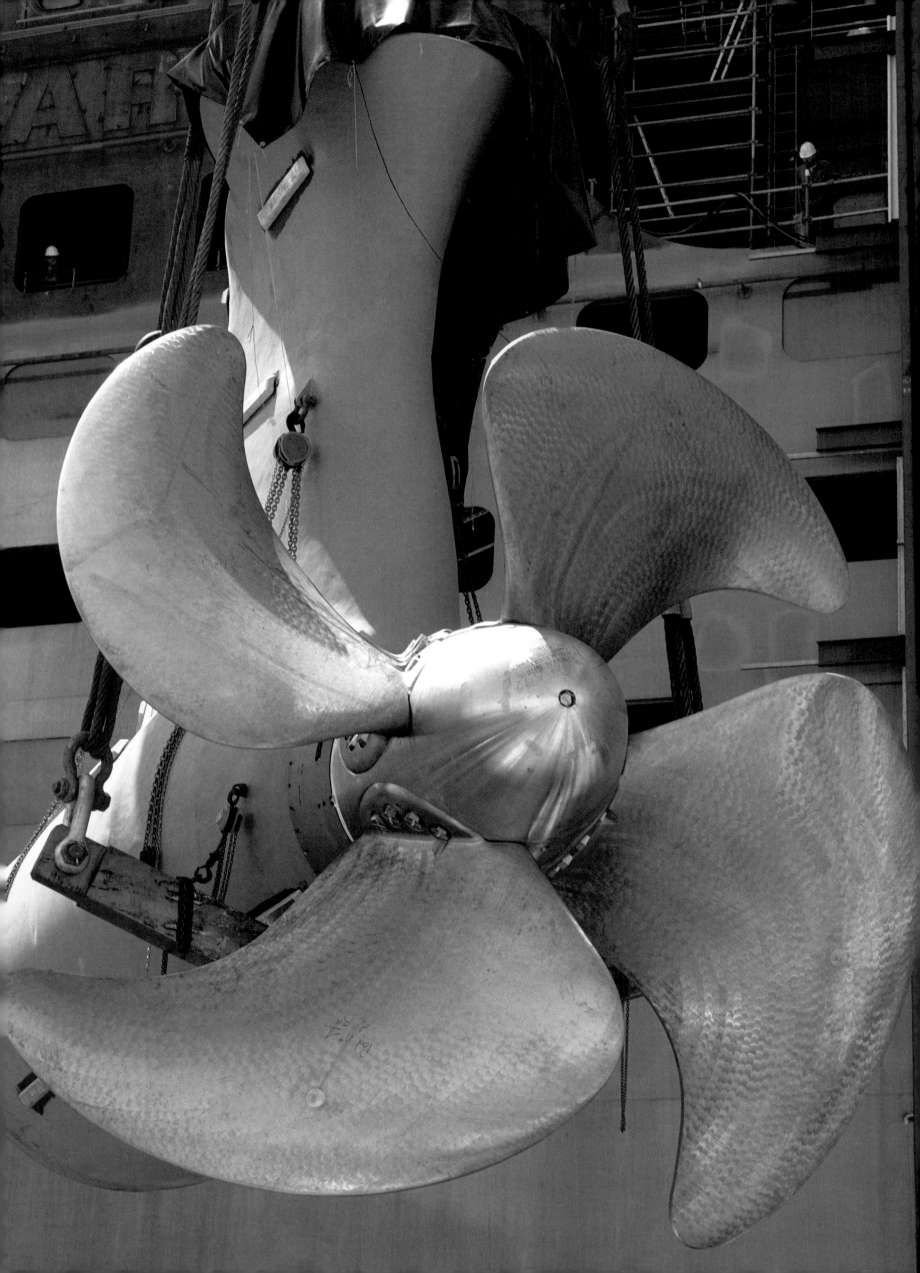

CUNARD

Despite today's bewildering output of new cruise ships, none has ever generated quite the same electrifying impact and excitement as the *Queen Mary 2*. No previous Cunarder ever assumed such astounding proportions and never before has a vessel of this magnitude and luxury entered service.

Queen Mary 2 is a true ocean liner, able to cross the daunting North Atlantic safely and swiftly year-round. Nothing like her has been launched since *Queen Elizabeth 2* first sailed in 1969. However splendid today's cruising vessels, none has the same reserves of power and reliability. And make no mistake about it, *Queen Mary 2*'s adaptability for world-class cruising has been superbly built-in as well.

Original *Queen Mary* was the first of her class, the model for all four of Cunard's *Queens*. She entered service back in 1936, sailing across an already troubled Atlantic; three years later, troopship *Queen Mary* started to embark millions of soldier/passengers, measurably hastening the completion of World War II before returning to peacetime service in 1946.

It was then that *Queen Mary* and her consort, *Queen Elizabeth*, came into their own, the most popular and successful passenger vessels ever to cross the Atlantic. Of the two, *Mary* attracted the strongest loyalty. Transatlantic passengers booked the same cabins repeatedly, not only to remeet an old friend but also to savor a luxurious seagoing experience.

Miraculously, *Queen Mary* is still with us. After thirty-one years of exemplary service, she avoided the scrap yard and is moored today at Long Beach as a floating hotel and museum. She remains the most beloved ocean liner of all time and, in show business terms, an extremely hard act to follow.

Thanks to the inspired, talented, and dedicated work of our Cunard family, I am pleased to report that second *Queen Mary* has emerged as the perfect successor, the promising descendent of that demanding original. I am convinced that this proud namesake will attract the same fierce passenger loyalty. She is far more than a mere re-creation of a beloved predecessor: *Queen Mary 2* is infinitely more innovative, boasting twenty-first-century options, amenities, and safety features undreamed in any Cunard predecessor. She also perfectly recaptures the grace and elegance of a bygone era, rewarding new generations of passengers with the transatlantic grandeur that so captivated their parents and grandparents.

In sum, *Queen Mary 2* is a vessel to astonish the world.

Micky Arison
Chairman, Carnival Corporation
(2003)

I first became interested in Cunard Line in the mid-1960s when my father was appointed Master Designate of *Queen Elizabeth 2*, then under construction in Scotland. At the time, I was Chief Officer aboard a freighter, and passenger ships were beyond my realm. That changed in 1969, when I boarded QE2 in Kingston, Jamaica. Her incredible grandeur and advanced technology amazed me, and it was immediately clear what kind of vessel I preferred.

I joined Cunard and, in April 1970, was appointed to stand by QE2 in Southampton's dry dock. My father went on leave the day I joined, so we only worked together that one day. On his return, I was appointed *Carmania*'s Third Officer.

After my father retired in 1972, I returned to QE2 and worked my way up the promotional ladder, subsequently commanding *Cunard Princess*, *Countess*, and *Dynasty*. Though my progress toward top post aboard *Queen Elizabeth 2* was steady, it often seemed in jeopardy. Cunard went through some tough economic times, and we feared the company might suffer the same demise as other North Atlantic lines.

Carnival Corporation took over Cunard in 1998 and, within months, announced their intention to build another *Queen*, to be called *Queen Mary 2*.

Until now, I always considered the highlight of my career appointment as master of *Queen Elizabeth 2* in 1990. Nothing, I thought, could top that. But in March 1998, I was privileged to be appointed as Master Designate of *Queen Mary 2*. And at the shipyard on July 4, 2002—exactly 162 years after little *Britannia*'s maiden voyage—I gave the command for QM2's keel to be laid.

Words cannot express the emotions I felt on both occasions, or my genuine pride about my long association with Cunard, a company that remains a dominant force throughout the cruise industry, with the only actual liners still sailing the North Atlantic.

As I write, our newest liner rests in the fitting-out basin, towering above the water. The designers' visions of grandeur and elegance are fast becoming a reality. Up on the bridge and down in the engine room alike, the very latest technological wizardry is being installed. The excitement grows daily.

I anxiously await sailing day so that *Queen Mary 2* can take her place on the world's oceans, upholding the traditions of the sea for which our Cunard Line is justly famous.

Commodore Ron W. Warwick
Master, *Queen Mary 2*
(2003)

Preface

This is the third Cunard history I have undertaken and, because of its extraordinary *raison d'être*, surely the most rewarding. The launch of the world's largest ocean liner at the start of the twenty-first century demands fullest documentation no less than admiration. *Queen Mary 2* is an incredible one-of-a-kind, a vessel to warm the hearts of every maritime historian and passenger alike. In shipyard lingo, "newbuilding" describes any ship under construction; this latest Cunard ocean liner embodies newbuilding of incomparable significance.

Of all contemporary cruise lines, Cunard boasts the most profound Anglo-American links. Founded by a Canadian, the Line and its steamers have served as palpable maritime connectors for 164 years, uniting mother country with former colony, the burgeoning, boisterous, and prosperous United States. Thanks to that historic traffic, Liverpool and Southampton remain inextricably twinned with New York. Make no mistake: Though Cunard's fleet was built, registered, and manned in Great Britain, the company's appeal no less than its major patronage has always been skewed unerringly toward America. Long before the English-Speaking Union was formally established in 1920, Samuel Cunard had laid the groundwork, forging geographical no less than emotional ties between Britons and Americans embarking aboard his company tonnage.

I must explain that, in the pages to follow, readers will find no more than passing reference to the company's heroic role throughout two world wars. The topic deserves a separate book; more importantly, ocean liners' wartime deployment remains the very antithesis of progress. However noble Cunard's response to both contingencies, brave crewmen and -women died and dozens of ships were destroyed. For merchant fleets, war is a brutal *force majeur* that puts growth on hold.

Whence my durable fascination with ocean liners? I can think of at least three cogent reasons. First, my Scottish kinsman Thomas Graham (later Lord Lynedoch) was the first passenger accommodated on the first steam-powered ocean liner. He embarked with his nephew Robert Graham aboard the American *Savannah* in Stockholm for passage to St. Petersburg in the fall of 1819.

Second, as the child of Scottish and American parents, it follows naturally that ocean crossings between Old World and New were rituals of my youth. Transatlantic travel became an addictive component of my life from the age of six months on.

Finally, I am reminded of a telling childhood experience at a Connecticut summer camp in August 1940. Two other boys and I were charged with delivering a huge cauldron of cocoa to an overnight camping site across the lake. We did so by rowboat, the steaming cocoa a simulacrum funnel amidships. As we rowed, I had with me a two-chime whistle with which we hooted our way through tendrils of nighttime mist. To impressionable eleven-year-olds—and a future maritime historian in particular—this was compelling ocean liner play, a haunting nocturnal voyage I have never forgotten, and irreplaceable fodder for an author/lecturer who, today, spends half his fortuitous life at sea.

The North Atlantic can be a daunting maritime arena, guaranteeing hard-fought passage across the most forbidding ocean of the world's seven. Winter storms are acknowledged as appalling but, as any transatlantic captain will advise you, unpredictable weather can be encountered every month of the year.

Small wonder that these trackless, turbulent wastes remain, indubitably and reassuringly, Cunard country.

John Maxtone-Graham
February 2004

BRITANNIA 1840–1848
1,135 grt. - 9 knots

PERSIA 1856–1867
3,300 grt. - 13.5 knots

SERVIA 1881–1901
7,392 grt. - 16 knots

UMBRIA 1884–1910
7,718 grt. - 19 knots

CAMPANIA 1893–1914
12,950 grt. - 21 knots

CARMANIA 1905–1931
19,524 grt. - 18 knots

LUSITANIA 1907–1915
31,550 grt. - 25 knots

MAURETANIA (I) 1907–1934
31,938 grt. - 25 knots

AQUITANIA 1914–1949
45,647 grt. - 23 knots

BERENGARIA 1920–1938
52,226 grt. - 22 knots

QUEEN MARY 1936–1967
81,237 grt. - 29 knots

MAURETANIA (II) 1939–1965
35,738 grt. - 23 knots

QUEEN ELIZABETH 1946–1968
83,673 grt. - 29 knots

CARONIA 1949–1967
34,183 grt. - 22 knots

QUEEN ELIZABETH 2 1969–
70,327 grt. - 28.5 knots

QUEEN MARY 2 2004–
150,000 grt. - 29.3 knots

The Giant in Prospect

*Perhaps, with your knowledge of North Atlantic liners,
you should try and arrive at your own design; only then
can we assess whether it makes economic sense.*

—Carnival Chairman Micky Arison, in preliminary conversation
with his naval architect Stephen Payne

Queen Mary 2 rose like a great gray behemoth from the bottom of Alstom Chantiers de l'Atlantique's longest dry dock.

Sprawling Alstom Chantiers de l'Atlantique is the central industrial complex of the town of St.-Nazaire, situated where the Loire debouches into the Atlantic. There, for more than a century and a half, an evocative parade of French Line tonnage has been produced. The patient, skilled hands of those Breton shipwrights gave life to immortals such as *Paris, Ile de France, Normandie,* and the third *France.*

In modern times, the yard continued its impeccable output, launching fleets of modern-day cruise ships. No more than five can be produced each year, a reflection of available dry-dock space as well as the yard's maximum capability of steel cutting and assembly. Suiting her stupefying dimensions, *Queen Mary 2* was assigned the logistical descriptive of "1.6 ships," yet another unique distinction for this gigantic Cunarder. But whatever their size, all newbuildings are conceived in the same manner. Every ship begins as a single pencil line drawn onto an otherwise blank sheet of drafting paper. From that simple beginning, a welter of additional lines—parallels, arcs, curves, angles, tangents, and grids—spreads across acres of paper. Simultaneously, those same designs proliferate into a profusion of computer databases. Thus is today's complex newbuilding web spun.

From the very outset, *Queen Mary 2* was destined to astonish, boasting every maritime superlative save two. She is the longest, broadest, and tallest passenger vessel ever launched, displacing a record 76,000 tons of water and with an unprecedented gross tonnage of 150,000 tons. Budgeted at nearly $800 million, she is also the most expensive. The only two superlatives eluding *QM2* are fastest—her power plant falls short of Blue Ribband, or record-breaking, performance—and her draft is shallower than her famous namesake's. But thanks to the combined muscle of a quartet of diesel alternators and twin gas turbines, she can tear along at thirty knots, in the glorious tradition of predecessor *Queens.*

With an overall length of 1,132 feet (345 meters), she comfortably surpasses the former world's longest *Norway-ex-France* by a hundred feet. Her 147-foot (45-meter) beam at the bridge betrays her as definitively —nay, *defiantly!*—too wide for Panama's canal. For this monster to circumnavigate the globe, it's either around Cape Horn or threading her way cautiously through the icy wastes of northern Canada's archipelago.

QM2's draft is 32 feet (10 meters), identical to that of current Cunard flagship *Queen Elizabeth 2* but less than the two original *Queens, Mary* and *Elizabeth,* whose whopping 42-foot (13-meter) draft sometimes necessitated waiting for flood tide in Southampton or New York. Draft is the only dimension that *QM2* and *QE2* share; in every other respect, this new flagship dwarfs her predecessor.

The visual impact of *Queen Mary 2*'s hull and super-structure—what her naval architect Stephen Payne describes succinctly as her "air draft"—amazes everyone, whether embarking passenger or envious, shore-bound spectator. From boot-topping to funnel top, she towers above the waterline 203 feet (62 meters), a remarkable elevation that alone separates her from every other vessel afloat. Incredible as it may seem, passengers sailing in and out of New York on the upper decks of this new Cunarder commune eye-to-eye with Lady Liberty.

However trippingly that cognomen—"new Cunarder" —falls off the tongue, it speaks volumes about *Queen Mary 2*'s long-overdue arrival. Indeed, after Carnival absorbed and restructured Cunard, the company was restyled as a two-ship brand—flagship *Queen Elizabeth 2* and *Vistafjord.* (Shortly thereafter, the latter was renamed *Caronia.*) No new purpose-built Cunarder has appeared for three decades. Not merely a new Cunarder, *QM2* is unquestionably the greatest Cunarder of all time. Moreover, *mirabile dictu,* she is imbued with the glorious but exacting specifications of an ocean liner.

Liners used to make line voyages—hence the name—from Old World to New in all seasons. They sailed year-round,

Opposite: *Queen Mary 2* under construction in Forme B, the yard's largest dry dock. Note how the bulbous bow still sports the brackets essential to its assembly.

through fair weather and foul, the very antithesis of today's shipboard-for-fun. Rather than pleasurable cruises, these were purposeful crossings. Whereas cruise ships dawdle around exotic itineraries, ocean liners persevere at speed, thundering across the world's most formidable oceans on bruising schedules.

The only other ocean liner extant is *Queen Elizabeth 2,* launched in 1967 and previously considered "the last Atlantic liner." Now Cunard has turned back the clock, rewriting history to duplicate and amplify those demanding criteria for *QM2.* Her dimensions and achievements should not be construed as hype, but mere hyperbole. The supplemental thickness of her forward hull plates, the number and stoutness of her ribs, the formidable structure of her bridge screen, and the massive, protective flare of her bows have all been wrought specifically to make her immune to the worst possible weather. So it is not only *Queen Mary 2's* landmark size, but her staunch, ocean liner genes that enshrine her forever in the record books.

Ships of any description do not just materialize. Their heritage evolves from prior company (or rival) tonnage and they come into being thanks to the dogged labor of thousands. In the vanguard is the visionary, who then seeks out experts—architect, engineer, shipbuilder, designer, planner, sailor, and administrator—and sets them to work. Their accumulated wisdom, experience, and toil are *Queen Mary 2's* life force, infusing shape, character, grace, and mobility into thousands of tons of inert steel.

Let us meet the principals behind this once-in-a-life-time mega-project. The visionary is unquestionably Micky Arison, chairman of Carnival Corporation. He surveys the world from a tenth-floor office at Carnival's Miami headquarters, outside of which an only slightly reduced replica of the company's signature red, white, and blue winged funnel has been installed in the midst of a flower bed.

Seated behind a U-shaped maple desk that belonged to his father, Arison is assured and ebullient, his beaming face adorned with rimless spectacles and a sandy moustache and goatee. At fifty-four, he is blessed with both the inspiration and the means to make extraordinary things happen in the shipping world.

Opposite: Inverted bottom sections for *Queen Mary 2* take shape in one of the yard's steel assembly sheds. *Above, left*: Carnival Corporation Chairman Micky Arison. *Above, right*: Cunard's admirable heritage, its maritime excellence exemplified by flagship *Queen Elizabeth 2,* made the company's purchase inevitable.

His late father Ted founded Carnival Cruises back in 1972 with a superannuated Canadian Pacific ocean liner called *Empress of Canada*; the original ship's bell stands in one corner of Micky's office, a potent Carnival talisman. Arison *père* rechristened her *Mardi Gras*, and, three remarkable decades after she first sailed out of Miami, Arison *fils* oversees an incredible floating empire, embracing a consolidated fleet of sixty-six vessels that produces annual revenues approaching seven billion dollars.

Carnival functions today as a benign maritime cooperative. Within that corporate fiefdom, cruise lines operate autonomously, dubbed in-house as the World's Leading Cruise Line Alliance. Participants include the vessels of Carnival Cruise Lines, Costa Cruises, Cunard Line, Holland America Line, P&O/Princess Cruises, Seabourn Cruises, and Windstar Cruises. The entire flotilla is made up of operators, ships, officers, and crews from around the world, marshaled into a giant consortium headquartered in Carnival's Miami office.

It was Micky Arison's bold decision to buy the historic but ailing British line from the Anglo-Norwegian Kvaerner conglomerate in 1998. For those who had contemplated Cunard on the block with disbelief, news that cruise purveyor Carnival had taken over the venerable transatlantic company seemed equally improbable. But in almost instant retrospective, Carnival's Cunard purchase made eminent good sense. Here at last was a refreshing infusion of cash, practicality, and drive. As Captain Ron Warwick said when he shared the news with his passengers in midocean aboard *Queen Elizabeth 2*: "We are all delighted to be owned once again by a shipping line rather than a hotel chain."

In fact, Arison had dreamed of a new ocean liner long before his Cunard purchase, suspecting that the historic company could serve as not only the perfect but also the only instrument of his ambition. "We bought Cunard," Arison says flat out, "to create *Queen Mary 2,* not the other way around." Nevertheless, Arison perceived the Cunard brand as a "hodgepodge," a fleet at odds with itself that boasted, regardless, an incomparable transatlantic heritage.

Arison and his colleagues were intrigued. "But what were we going to do with it?" he reflects today. "This was

around the time of the *Titanic* movie. We were all talking about this overwhelming nostalgia movement in the country. What if we built the next great ocean liner?" I'm fascinated that the fabled White Star liner had contributed its potent mystique into the mix and set Arison and Carnival on the road to acquisition and construction. Moreover, the potent lure of the name "White Star" was not lost on Arison, following the success of the *Titanic* film. The White Star suffix—half the company name of Cunard White Star dating from their 1932 merger—had been dropped by Cunard in the early fifties. Resuscitated and trademarked, it could only enhance Cunard's present-day image of high-end luxe.

Of the dozens of newbuildings that Micky Arison has ushered into service, none was more challenging or ambitious than the vessel he envisioned as Cunard's replacement flagship. Arison was determined to burnish anew Cunard's historic transatlantic crown, recapturing for a new generation of passengers the seagoing grandeur that had so enchanted their parents and grandparents. In the chairman's own words: "*Queen Mary 2* will carry the grace and elegance of a bygone era into the future."

As a visionary anxious to implement his dream and explore its technical feasibility, Arison had the right expert in-house. A pivotal member of Carnival's newbuilding team is Stephen Payne, a brilliant young naval architect, the oldest of four brothers and a born and bred Londoner.

Payne has been intimately involved with a succession of Carnival newbuildings since his initial employment by UK shipbuilding consultants TMP (Technical Marine Planning) in 1985. In that capacity, he was involved with designing Carnival's *Holiday* and, later, the company's *Fantasy*-class, its first vessel delivered in 1990.

Following Carnival's 1989 acquisition of Holland America Line, Payne was immersed in the *Statendam*-class sextet. In 1992, he moved on to Carnival's *Destiny*-class, followed three years later by assignment as project manager for Holland-America's *Rotterdam VI*. That same year, 1995, Carnival absorbed TMP into its permanent newbuilding team.

Payne is blessed in that his rewarding profession crystallized from a childhood obsession. An episode from the television program *Blue Peter* first fired the seven-year-old

viewer's imagination. Footage from a *Queen Elizabeth* 1967 Channel crossing conveyed the majesty of the Cunarder's great hull as well as the size and grandeur of her public rooms; Stephen was instantly hooked. In 1969, Cunard invited the public aboard to inspect brand-new *Queen Elizabeth 2*, and, not surprisingly, the Payne family, on holiday in nearby Bournemouth, came up to Southampton to see her for themselves.

A January 1972 *Blue Peter* broadcast captured live images of Payne's beloved *Queen Elizabeth* afire in Hong Kong harbor. In the program's *Blue Peter Annual*, published later that year, a writer hazarded that a liner of comparable size would never again be built. Payne recalls, "I wrote to the program to say that I thought they were wrong and that one day there might be. I still have their reply, wishing me well and hoping that such a vision might some day come true. Well, the rest is history!"

A top-ranked schoolboy debater, Payne is a formidable speaker. He speaks with fluent assurance, patently in love with his subject and devastatingly well-informed, as authoritative as he is articulate.

Physically, Payne is an Englishman's Englishman, of medium height with a beaming, almost Dickensian visage; wire-rimmed spectacles frame eyes of bemused intensity. His platform style is essentially academic—meticulous but never dull—the words delivered with a pungent South London accent. He punctuates points with spare, disciplined gestures, enlivening potentially dry passages with flashes of deadpan humor.

Amongst the revealing graphics he enjoyed screening when introducing *Queen Mary 2* to audiences was his overlay of comparative Cunard profiles. Lower left, looking like a toy, is *Britannia* of 1840, the Cunard *alpha* for which *QM2* serves as crowning *omega*. Outlined as well are present-day flagship *QE2* and the first *Queen Mary*, a veritable giant of her time. But *QM2*'s vast footprint eclipses them all.

The genesis of what became *Queen Mary 2* was unconventional. Traditionally, when a naval architect is asked to design a newbuilding for an owner, he responds with three essential questions: How many passengers? How fast? How luxurious? But this was no conventional assignment;

Above, left: Queen Mary 2's inspired naval architect Stephen Payne. *Above, right:* First *Queen Elizabeth* was the vessel that most impressed Payne as a child. *Opposite:* Dwarfed by engine-room machinery, a welder plies his dazzling trade.

Queen Mary 2

Arison was obliged to reverse the order of things. Before providing capacity, speed, or lavishness, he needed informed guidance. Nothing approaching the specifications for the vessel about which he fantasized had been tackled before. Hard data would only emerge after some arduous new research. So, in an understandable role reversal, naval architect Payne would ultimately define for owner Arison the exacting maritime parameters he sought.

To that end, Payne was instructed to embark on an extensive study as to what form a viable and economically sound twenty-first-century ocean liner should take. Arison concluded his brief with two wry caveats: "Stephen, in your lifetime, you will only have one opportunity to design such a ship so you had better get it right the first time!"

Moments later, the chairman added: "After this ship, I don't quite know what I am going to give you to follow on. Nothing will ever compare with this."

For the naval architect, it was a flattering, albeit sobering, moment. Payne was gratefully aware that he had been entrusted with contemporary shipbuilding's dream commission. Project *Queen Mary 2* was under way.

His formal research began in May 1998. He and colleague Richard Moore embarked on an exhaustive two-year study. One inescapable mantra guided Payne from the beginning: "You cannot place a ship in regular North Atlantic service in the near winter months unless you have a true liner." He is haunted by the ordeal of the Italian Line's *Michelangelo* during a westbound crossing in April 1966. Patently, her bridge screen had been inadequately constructed. As she was being driven fast through a storm to New York, a monster wave struck the fore part of the ship, and two passengers and a crewman were killed. Payne was determined that his *Queen Mary 2* should achieve epic invulnerability.

Of necessity, every liner shares several essential characteristics: high speed, buttoned-up superstructure, a long bow deck, engines amidships, lifeboats high above the waterline, deep draft, and a finely shaped hull. Few if any contemporary newbuildings meet those relentless criteria. Standard cruising speed seldom exceeds twenty knots, top hampers tower high above the sea and are crowded forward,

draft is restricted for tug-free, in-port maneuvering, and, between finely wrought bow and stern, hulls are consistently flat. Since today's ships are assembled from prefabricated sections, or blocks, keeping most of those giant Lego pieces stolidly rectangular makes economic sense.

Admittedly, some cruise ships destined for global deployment share some ocean liner proclivities. One such was *Oriana* of 1995. She boasted a service speed of twenty-five rather than twenty-two knots. Additionally, owners P & O required that the vessel exhibit what are called good sea-keeping characteristics, capable of coping with weather more demanding than that encountered in the placid Caribbean.

By the same token, when designing the sixth *Rotterdam,* Payne and the shipyard modified *Statendam*'s basic hull shape into something approaching a liner. He not only added length to derive an economical turn of speed, but also made the hull less boxy. By so doing, he sacrificed some stability but made it up by increasing her beam. Since *Rotterdam* would be faster than *Statendam,* she would have to carry more fuel, so Payne increased her draft for additional bunker capacity.

But those refinements did not make *Rotterdam* a real liner. No legitimate ocean liner had been built since *QE2* of 1969. Faced with the task of designing one more than thirty years after the last one had been built, Payne was fully aware that shipbuilding has changed radically since 1969. Today's passenger expectations are quite different; moreover, a contemporary ocean liner would be notoriously expensive to build and to operate.

Incidentally, there was scant useful input from the world's shipyards. Helsinki's Kvaerner Masa's had submitted a preliminary, ostensible ocean liner design, siting a large dining room aft, directly above the propellers. The Finns were obviously locked into a placid, cruising mindset quite inadequate for the rigors of North Atlantic service. As it happened, Payne's ultimate decision was to position *QM2*'s dining rooms nearer stern than bow, close to what he describes as the "center of pitch."

Something similar to *QE2* was the obvious answer. But whereas St.-Nazaire categorizes the size of *QM2* as "1.6 of a ship," she would represent 1.4 of a ship in financial

Opposite: Fitting with the exactitude of a giant jigsaw puzzle piece, a stern section is lowered carefully into place. *Above*: Hard hats and drawings are inescapable shipyard leitmotivs.

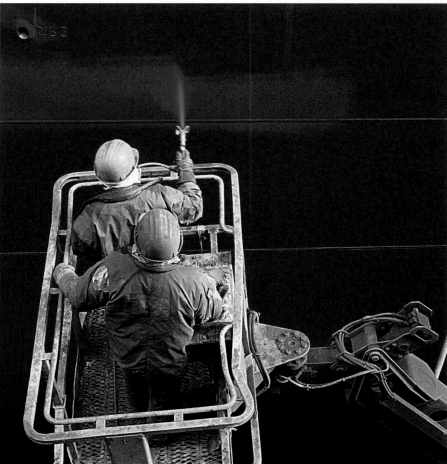

terms. Meeting ocean liner specifications involved a daunting 40 percent price differential. The power required to drive the vessel at speed, the increased thickness, strength, and weight of structural components, and, not to be ignored, the potential loss of revenue within a shaped rather than a boxy hull had to be factored in. Regardless of those additional costs, Payne's finished design would have to pass muster with the hard-boiled pragmatists of Carnival's accounting department.

One of his earliest tasks was to analyze *QE2*'s thirty-year track record; "Building on positives and rejecting things that don't work" remains a firm Payne philosophy that has paid dividends over the years. Similarly, he is never not evaluating maritime successes and failures, continually reappraising the ups and downs of merchant ship history.

Since he had sailed as a *QE2* passenger many times, Payne was extremely familiar with her interior design. He found, for example, her staircase system "immensely confusing," an inevitable result of conflicting planning decisions when she was built. Originally designed for three classes, *QE2* entered service hastily modified for two; nowadays, her passenger load is accommodated essentially within a single class. Had the vessel been designated as

such from the outset, her entire arrangement would have been different.

Additionally, the presumed wraparound, enclosed promenade had been incorporated within public rooms instead. Passengers tramping around the open-air promenade up on the boat deck cannot easily complete a circuit around the ship's forward end because of a staircase and elevated, open-air lookout that is untenable in high winds.

The vessel's structural details offered cautionary hindsight as well. *QE2*'s top five decks are fabricated entirely of aluminum. (She was launched, in fact, with three superstructure decks already in place.) This involved an enormous plus for the ship's stability, allowing inclusion of one more deck than if her superstructure had been fabricated of steel alone. In this configuration, *QE2* was, when built, the largest passenger ship able to traverse the Panama Canal.

Nevertheless, in the long term, aluminum involves some disadvantages. Though one-sixth the weight of steel, it is less dense and it hardens with age, changing characteristics. After more than three decades, *QE2*'s superstructure has lost much of its initial resiliency. Panels of the metal around the upper three decks are starting to show

Above: Clydeside workers paint original *Queen Mary*'s hull by hand. These days, paint is sprayed on. *Opposite*: Stephen Payne determined that the solution for the vessel's after end is the "Constanzi" stern, combining both cruiser and transom sterns.

wear. Cracking has occurred at stress points—around window frames, in corners, and even where holes have been drilled. Since aluminum cannot be easily strapped or patched, occasional panels have been replaced.

This prompted one of Payne's earliest decisions: *QM2* should be of all steel construction, a resolve that carried potent ramifications, particularly in the matter of size. By substituting five aluminum with five steel decks, it was clear that he would end up with a ship smaller than *QE2*, because stability requirements meant that he would be obliged to have one less deck.

Conversely, the economics of the project demanded that *QM2* could not be smaller than *QE2*; it had to be not only as big, but bigger. Indeed, the inevitability of that mammoth expansion was guaranteed throughout the study as Arison added marketing demands into the technological mix. An extract from Payne's notes encapsulates *QM2*'s growth progress succinctly: "Size determination, including review of aluminum superstructure on *QE2* allowing Panamax vessel of 70,000 grt, economy of scale and all steel design leading to post Panamax 150,000 grt." (The abbreviation "grt" stands for "gross registered tonnage." "Panamax" describes the largest hull capable of transiting Panama's 1,000-foot by 110-foot [305-meter by 34-meter] locks; post Panamax characterizes vessels prohibited by size from doing so.)

It took the *Queen Mary* project team a full two and a half years to complete their task. In Stephen Payne's words, "We estimated powering, ship weight to almost 1,500 tonnes accuracy, etc. etc., all from adapting data from *QE2* and our own knowledge." The team achieved a monumental triumph. When their data were inspected by the shipyard's naval architects, they were adjudged compellingly complete.

Not the least of their difficulties was that Carnival's management kept requesting greater passenger capacity as well as a higher ratio of cabins with balconies. No sooner had those amendments been incorporated and resubmitted than further increases were requested. Like Alice in Wonderland, *Queen Mary 2* "grew and grew" as the preliminary design expanded to qualify as not only magnificent but also a money-earner. In this way, the

Opposite: In the dry dock, or Forme B, lifeboat davits have been set in place above the starboard promenade. *Above*: QE2 was launched with much of her aluminum superstructure in place.

vessel's height, beam, and length increased to their present record-breaking dimensions.

In point of fact, the only limitations to a ship's size are twofold: her overall length must allow her sufficient maneuvering room within home port and ports of call. As regards height, she must pass beneath every bridge spanning every itinerary.

QM2's overall length of 1,132 feet (345 meters) creates no problem in Southampton. The Queen Elizabeth II terminal where she ties up between transatlantic voyages boasts a generous quay front that encompasses her length without difficulty. Moreover, the port's lower turning basin immediately offshore is large enough to allow the vessel's routine inbound maneuver. Arriving at dawn off the terminal, *QM2* executes a complete 180-degree turn before docking portside, bow pointing downharbor in anticipation of that evening's departure. According to Southampton senior pilot Bill Range, there is a more than adequate radius of 1,500 feet (457 meters) between the berth and a limiting channel marker near the opposite shore, identified—with good reason—as the Hythe Knock. Then too, pilots have a reserve contingency: if additional maneuvering space is required, a pilot can intrude *Queen Mary 2*'s bow over the threshold of the adjacent capacious ocean dock, the now-unused passenger facility where predecessor *Queen*s once berthed.

In New York Harbor, length is not a problem either, although 34 feet (10-plus meters) of second *Queen Mary*'s hull jut out beyond the end of the 1,100-foot (335-meter) passenger-ship terminal's finger piers. Similarly, there is sufficient room out in the channel when she backs out of the slip to turn downriver for departure.

Most challenging is the arrival, as inbound *QM2* pauses at pier's end. There she must negotiate a 90-degree starboard turn, pointing her bow due east for entry into the 400-foot (122-meter) wide New York slip. This can be a demanding maneuver when spring runoff from upstate buttresses the Hudson's downriver flow, making arduous the northward swing of the vessel's huge stern.

Rather than length, New York's prohibitive limitation is height. *Queen Mary 2*'s formidable 203-foot (62-meter) air draft is the maximum permissible. Payne had to restrict

the elevation of both mast and funnel top in order to leave ten feet (three-plus meters) of clearance below the roadway of the Verrazzano Narrows Bridge. As he jests ruefully, "If we haven't got it right, it will only be a problem the first time; either the bridge or the funnel will disappear."

Once his vessel's parameters had been finalized, Payne had next to determine whether the design met or, preferably, surpassed the demands he knew it would encounter in service. Those answers could only be revealed within the confines of a model-testing tank. Carnival's chosen facility was MARIN (Maritime Research Institute), founded in the early 1930s. Europe's largest deepwater and offshore testing facility, it is located in the Netherlands' town of Wageningen, near Arnhem. MARIN recently celebrated testing its eight-thousandth hull, an enviable achievement.

The facility's primary function is to prove design feasibility, bridging the gap between well-reasoned theory and hard-nosed practicality. MARIN's technical director, Reint Dallinga, puts it as follows, prefacing his remarks with a wry assessment of his company's travails:

"In the financial stress-field between owner and builder, MARIN supplies an 'assurance' of the vessel's speed in trial conditions, its maneuvering characteristics, and its ability to maintain speed and course at sea in service conditions."

Over much of the year 2000, two scrupulously wrought, yellow models of the *Queen Mary 2* hull—one large and one smaller—were built and tested at MARIN. These were the first actual three-dimensional replicas, however small, of the giant vessel itself. Both betrayed the brute strength and pronounced flare of the real ship's bows, reminiscent of both *Queen Elizabeth 2* and the original *Queen Mary*. But because three decks of cabin balconies are incorporated within the hull, Payne had amplified the protective flare of his forward steel hull plates to divert oncoming waves more efficiently to either side.

In turn, each model was launched into MARIN's largest tank, a giant, indoor cement trough nearly 600 feet (180 meters) long, 131 feet (40 meters) wide, and 16 feet (5 meters) deep. Once afloat, the larger *QM2* model was attached by a rigid towing bridle to a carriage that spanned the tank and rode on twin rail tracks along either side.

First towed by the carriage to determine resistance, then subsequently self-propelled to ascertain powering requirements, the model's form was continually refined to improve performance. For subsequent sea-keeping tests, the smaller of the two models was employed, detached from the tow but linked to the carriage by a multiconductor umbilical cord. Equipped with both propellers and stabilizers, this smaller model could be propelled and steered from "shore" by radio command.

The tank's water can be roiled to produce any sea conditions, from a force-two breeze to fearsome rollers. Thus, models can be made to pitch (the bow rising and falling), roll (rocking from side to side), or scend, a diabolical combination of the two. For days, as computers monitored her performance, *QM2*'s hull was run at varying speeds through a gauntlet of increasingly ominous sea conditions.

The bow configuration proved admirable. Persevering at twenty knots through simulated, hurricane-sized waves, the prow negotiated approaching juggernauts superbly, shrugging potential inundations aside.

Next, it was necessary to find out if the vessel's stern matched the efficiency of the bow. The smaller *QM2* model was liberated from the towing bridle and waves were generated to impact the stern.

Early in the design phase, Payne had debated incorporating a planing surface into his underwater stern. A planing surface—an arbitrary expanse of flat steel beneath the counter—encourages a hull to rise and literally plane across the sea. Such a refinement had contributed to *United States*'s

What's in a bow? *Above*: QE2 in midocean and model *QM2* in a tank negotiate testing waves. *Opposite*: Design components from the original *Mary* and QE2 helped shape *QM2*'s bow.

phenomenal performance back in 1952 when she won the Blue Ribband.

But planing surfaces involve a cautionary catch-22: Speed may be improved but at the cost of a more vulnerable stern. As a result, Payne's final design combined a modified transom with elements of the first *Queen Mary*'s cruiser stern; described as the "Constanzi stern," a similar arrangement had been pioneered for *Oceanic* and *Eugenio C* in the mid-1960s. The hybrid was necessary because a simple transom stern, slapped by a following sea, can set up troublesome vibrations the length of a hull. But the *Queen Mary 2* version had to be further refined to provide appropriate "landing spaces" for her propellers.

The model's four working stabilizers were located as on the full-scale prototype—two a side amidships. Payne and MARIN were both anxious to know not only how they would perform during damp rolling, but also what corrective effect they could exert with a following sea.

Subjected to a wave onslaught from astern, model *QM2* exhibited what is described as a 'hunting instinct': The hull cycled through a series of random, side-slipping undulations. When those waves were amplified, the movement was so pronounced that propellers tended to emerge above water. The solution was installation of a remedial skeg—a stout vertical steel divider separating the two aftermost propellers. That skeg, in combination with the stabilizers, minimized the hunting instinct and vastly improved *QM2*'s longitudinal stability in a following sea.

Mention of "the two aftermost propellers" tips my hand. This is obviously the moment for preliminary discussion of the remarkable propulsion system of the *Queen Mary 2*. She is the first quadruple-screwed vessel to appear on the North Atlantic since *France* of 1962. Employment of four propellers was *sine qua non* for all giant twentieth-century Cunarders from *Lusitania* on up to but not including *Queen Elizabeth 2*, which has only two. But *Mauretania, Aquitania, Berengaria,* and both predecessor *Queens* joined *QM2* in boasting four. The view over the second *Queen Mary*'s stern reveals the same broad wake that furrowed the North Atlantic in the old days.

But apart from their number, everything else about *QM2*'s propeller quartet is radically different. To start

Opposite: Arriving in Forme C aboard multiwheeled transporter, the first Mermaid pod is lofted up by crane. *Above:* The pod is about to be transferred from crane slings to cables extended through the hull that will snug it up into position.

with, the vessel's "engine room" is not even inside the vessel. Each propeller, as well as the huge electric motor driving it, is part of a separate pod suspended beneath the hull. Though the two forward pods are fixed, the after two rotate through 360 degrees, obviating the need for a rudder. Initially, provision had been made for a rudder, but tests indicated that it would have to have been so huge that unacceptable drag would have resulted. So there is no rudder whatsoever; *QM2* is steered instead by her two azimuthal pods.

The electrical power required to drive the vessel's propellers comes from two sources, the first of which is four diesel generators positioned low down in the vessel amidships. Their uptakes to the funnel have been divided, in the manner of *Vaterland, Normandie,* and *Nieuw Amsterdam.* Rather than disrupt passenger access along the keel line, the chimneys connecting generator room with funnel adhere port and starboard to the quarter-width sides of the hull, leaving an unobstructed central thoroughfare connecting public rooms.

Two additional engines produce even more electricity. These are twenty-five-kilowatt gas turbines, sited high in

the vessel where they not only have convenient access to the huge volumes of air they require but also obviate the need for additional uptake casings. Concealed within both sides of the funnel's base, each is chambered within a soundproof enclosure. That pair, in concert with the four alternators below, churns out sufficient kilowatts to meet all of *QM2*'s engine and service electricity needs. Their combined output could power a city the size of Southampton.

Payne's hull passed her MARIN tests with flying colors, Reint Dallinga's daunting "financial stress-field" successfully negotiated and fullest "assurance" guaranteed.

Now to document Payne's upper deck choices. Some fellow architects and ocean liner aficionados had hoped that the second *Queen Mary* might be topped with multiple funnels similar to the trio adorning her famous namesake. Why not enhance Arison's commitment to steamship nostalgia by replicating that beloved profile with three stacks—genuine or dummy—perhaps with lounges incorporated into their structures?

But Payne never even considered it, quick to point out that for every ton of top weight, two tons must be added below decks. Moreover, he likely felt but did not articulate that cluttering the vessel with fake special effects would vitiate the purity of his design. *Queen Mary 2* is, after all, neither a styled cruising fantasy nor a whimsical retro reproduction. Rather, she is a valid ocean liner, a serious creation that, uncompromisingly constructed, must

How shipbuilding has changed: Above: In 1938, the first Queen Elizabeth would thunder down fixed ways into the Clyde. Opposite: Second Queen Mary floated quietly off the dry dock floor.

CHANTIERS

convey a maximum of 2,800 passengers safely and comfortably at speed in all weathers. Payne was determined that nothing should sully his profile. "To my knowledge," he ruminates, "though they may have inherited some, Cunard never built a liner with a dummy funnel. So why do so now?"

That said, he did succumb to some minor upper deck fakery, an ingenious *trompe l'oeil* device adorning the corners of his bridge screen. (The bridge screen is the forward end of every vessel's superstructure, the maritime equivalent of an automotive hood and windshield.) By application of two decks' worth of horizontal, wraparound black lines, Payne has visually recapitulated the look of the original *Queen Mary*'s forward deck crossovers.

Structurally, the second *Queen Mary*'s bridge screen emerged as an intricately wrought marvel, form adhering faithfully to function. It radiates strength and reliability, what the French express so eloquently with the single word *puissance*. So compelling is its complexity of curves, a traditional bowed front (*Queen Mary 1* again) that slopes as well, cone-shaped, rising to the formidable brow of the bridge and doubly convex for strength. Perhaps most distinctive are its stout corners, gracefully sloping brackets that tie all superstructure decks together while incorporating yet another audacious curve—concave, this time—into the mix of planes. Those robust shoulders define and encapsulate the entire structure. Overall, *Queen Mary 2* has been blessed with a forward-facing façade that proclaims

itself immune to the worst possible seas. Would that poor *Michelangelo* had boasted such an enviable forward rampart!

By way of bewitching contrast, immediately aft of each bridge screen corner, an exterior panoramic elevator provides a delicate, illuminated verticality. At the bottom of the bridge screen's slope are two resonances from another of Payne's ocean liner favorites, the French Line's 1935 *Normandie*. The white steel arc of a whaleback conceals the forward mooring machinery, and a stout, V-shaped breakwater—shaped like an inverted locomotive's snowplow—serves as a supplementary line of defense against encroaching seas.

Amidships, *QM2*'s overriding profile feature is her towering single funnel. To either side, its base is cradled within the twin, curved, aerodynamic flumes that elevate and disperse stack gas well over the stern. The entire funnel structure, although distinctive and more massive, renders homage to the predecessor flagship, extending Cunard's contemporary design continuum.

But there is not a shred of *QE2* continuum the length of *QM2*'s flanks. Here instead is a formidably up-to-date commitment: Superstructure and hull are perforated with row after row of balconies. Their presence *in extenso* cogently underscores Stephen Payne's appreciation of how much shipboard has changed since *QE2* first appeared in 1969. Not one cabin balcony had been incorporated into her original configuration. Admittedly, balconied suites, in the form of prefabricated, aluminum modules, have been attached to her upper decks over the years.

Opposite: The overwhelming bulk of Stephen Payne's bridge bloc descends into place. *Above: QM2*'s chic single stack seems light-years removed from original *Mary*'s dignified trio.

Outdoor cabin access aboard *QE2* is restricted, perforce, to occupants of the vessel's most rarified accommodations. By way of exhilarating contrast, no fewer than eight *QM2* decks are festooned with balconies. (In fact, Arison had requested seven but Payne upped the ante with an additional deck's worth.) The bottom three balcony rows are inset (uniquely) within the hull itself, at a secure remove from the bow. The incredible result is that fully three quarters of *Queen Mary 2's* cabins come complete with open-air terraces overlooking the sea.

The two most palatial balconied suites—appropriately named Sandringham and Balmoral—are double-deckers occupying the after corners of the superstructure on Decks 9 and 10. The visual effect of the terraced descent of her five after levels, from Deck 12 down to Deck 7 (strength), is yet again reminiscent of *QE2's* stepped profile. Payne has sloped all their protective windscreens—mullions and glass alike—with a forward-facing, streamlined rake, imparting a dynamic urgency to the vessel's after end.

With hull and general arrangement completed and approved, the next step was for shipyards to submit their tenders to build *Queen Mary 2*. This happened on June 4, 1999. Kiel's HDW yard bowed out, confessing that the project was just too big. Similarly, the excellent German yard at Pappenberg could not qualify because of the fixed, restrictive dimensions of their permanent building shed. Finland's MASA yard was extremely interested but pre-ordained building schedules forbade it; their capacious Turku dry docks on the country's west coast had been preempted by Royal Caribbean International *Voyager*-class newbuildings. Similarly, Italy's Monfalcone order book was full of Princess and Carnival Destiny tonnage. Closer to home, the venerable Belfast yard of Harland & Wolff had internal financing limitations that could not accommodate the scale of the *QM2* undertaking.

The French won out. A letter of intent with Alstom Chantiers de l'Atlantique at St.-Nazaire was signed in March of 2000 and in November, a final building contract certified delivery for December 2003.

Here was a double first: A *Queen* to be constructed outside the United Kingdom and a Cunarder to be built in France. Britain's traditional shipbuilding preeminence had tragically eroded. In 1886, 151 steamers were built on the Clyde alone; today, only one Clyde-side shipyard remains extant.

This moment conjures up the opening vision of this chapter. The vessel's optimum shape had been determined, its steel shell perfected. Stephen Payne was not only pleased with his creation, he was also supremely confident of its groundbreaking qualifications. "*Queen Mary 2*," he declared, "is probably the strongest and most adequately designed transatlantic liner to date." An additional bonus was that the vessel be imbued with what he described as "a forty-year fatigue life." Although North Atlantic liners traditionally anticipated a thirty-year life expectancy, Payne was adamant that *Queen Mary 2*—his superliner, if you will—comfortably exceed every prior expectation.

The next step was for Cunard and its appointed interior designers to decorate and furnish every corner of their giant steel structure. Having examined *QM2's* exterior, it is time to meet Cunard's management and their chosen designers before embarking into the belly of the beast.

Above: Shipyard workers are inveterate bicyclists, and parking is no problem. *Opposite*: An overview of sections-in-waiting along *l'aire de prémontage* and adjoining Forme B.

Opposite: The bulbous bow complete, bow sections above it are still open to the skies. *Above:* Down these emerging twin stair-cases over the years to come, thousands of *QM2* passengers will descend to dine. *Overleaf:* A panoramic view of *QM2* in Forme B reveals the section joints: wherever platform rows adhere to the vessel's sloping sides, exterior welds are being completed.

Above: A haunting view of G32 juxtaposed against St-Nazaire's suspension bridge spanning the Loire. *Opposite*: A pair of welders work intently within segregated steel compartments of an over-turned bottom section.

Cunard Enrichment

When you first you come on board, if you half-close your eyes, you will sense immediately that you are on a liner from the twenties or thirties. But open them fully and you will realize at once that the décor is also strikingly contemporary.

—Fredrik Johanssen, Tillberg Design

Only when every square inch of *Queen Mary 2*'s dimensions had been approved could Payne hand over the final "block form" GA (general arrangement) to those charged with cladding and finishing her interiors and deckscapes. Too many of today's vessels, he feels, are designed by interior architects who "create their own idealized general arrangement and then rely on the naval architect and marine engineers to make it all work." Payne was happy that, in this event, matters proceeded by the book. He, as naval architect, perfected every interior parameter before relinquishing the vessel to Cunard for the next design phase.

That work began in April 1999. Through the auspices of their selected designers, the character and décor of every cabin, public room, staircase, deck, and alleyway would be established. It was a lengthy and complex process, as demanding as Payne's initial design chores. Three and a half years' worth of logistical, practical, and aesthetic choices had to be made: a continuous selecting, winnowing, and approval process that extended right up to delivery day in December 2003.

The collaboration was, perforce, a thoroughly international process, in marked contrast to the old days. The first *Queen Mary* was constructed during the 1930s at Scotland's historic Clydeside shipyard of John Brown. Not surprisingly, since the vessel was being completed with a hard-won parliamentary subsidy, almost every supplier and vendor was British. Structural components, engineering material, machinery, pumps, chandlery, decking, carpeting, fabrics, and furnishings arriving at John Brown's originated almost exclusively within the United Kingdom.

But more than six decades later, contemporary newbuildings are wrought from suppliers spread throughout a global marketplace. The *Queen Mary 2* is equipped with propellers and tapestries from Poland, gas turbines from Texas, chairs and tables from Italy, diesel engines from Denmark, pods from France, and bridge controls from Germany. Among British firms adding to the mix are Glasgow's Brown Brothers for the four stabilizers, Rolls Royce for the pods' motors, bow-thrusters, and deck machinery, and a variety of UK subcontractors for many of the vessel's electrical systems.

And as with vendors, so too the entire sequence of design selection and execution transcended national boundaries. Whereas Payne and his team had completed their hull research in London, it was tested, as we have seen, in Holland. While the vessel would be built in France, the choices dictating her interior look would coalesce from a joint international effort divided amongst Florida, Sweden, Holland, St.-Nazaire, and London.

Cunard's head office was relocated from its traditional Manhattan venue south to Florida in 1997. A year later, the company was fully acquired by Carnival. These days, Cunard occupies several floors of a verdantly landscaped office tower along Blue Lagoon Drive, hard by Miami Airport. Leading Cunard Line is Pamela Conover, a Carnival alumnae who was appointed COO in 1998 and president in 2001.

Although her arrival at Cunard coincided with the planning for history's largest ocean liner, an extensive shipping apprenticeship proved ideal preparation. Indeed, earlier career choices seemed presciently apropos for the task at hand, an opportunity that she relishes. Throughout her life, President Conover has consistently met and overcome demanding challenges head-on.

Conover was born in Bangkok in 1956, the second of four children of a British trading company executive. From the beginning, her childhood impacted with shipping. She and her siblings sometimes embarked with their father on inspection tours of visiting ships anchored off Pattaya. Indeed, an overview of Conover's life reveals two dominant threads, a career fabric woven inextricably with financial warp and maritime woof.

After working as a teller at the London office of Wells Fargo Bank, Conover requested a transfer to Wells Fargo's New York office where she studied to become a credit

Above: A trove of brand-new Wedgwood plates ready to go on board. *Opposite*: A famous poster from 1933 flaunts not only future *Queen Mary*'s imposing funnels but also betrays the merger of Cunard with White Star.

Can you wait?

analyst. Her maiden venture into the shipping world was as assistant treasurer for the container shipping company United States Lines.

In the mid-1980s, Conover moved on to Citicorp, appointed vice-president of—what else?—the ship financing department. In 1992, she was promoted to managing director of the company's entire North American ship-financing business.

Not surprisingly, one of Citicorp's foremost clients was Carnival Corporation. Conover played a pivotal role in securing financing for a surge of fleet expansions, Carnival's among them. One of her first jobs as department head was stage managing Carnival's Seabourn acquisition.

Two years later, when Carnival invested in Epirotiki Cruise Lines, Conover was invited to become president and CEO of the eastern Mediterranean carrier. And when Carnival divested itself of Epirotiki in 1995, Conover was invited to come aboard at Carnival, assigned the post of vice-president for strategic planning. It was that position that served as springboard for her Cunard posting, first as chief operating officer under former president Larry Pimentel, then as president following his resignation.

Conover's right hand at Cunard is Deborah Natansohn, who holds the pivotal position of senior vice-president for sales and marketing. Over the course of her career, New Yorker Natansohn has profited from a wealth of in-depth travel and cruise experience.

After graduating from State University of New York, Albany in 1974, Natansohn took a post with *Trade Travel* magazine before moving on for a five-year stint as marketing director for Travellers International, where her clients included TWA Getaway, SAS Viking Vacations, and, significantly, Cunard Europe tour programs. She also spent three years as director of marketing for the Arthur Frommer travel organization.

Subsequently, Natansohn was immersed within the hands-on administration of various cruise lines, serving as vice-president for marketing at both Ocean Cruise Lines and Pearl Cruises, and later as senior vice-president for Orient Lines. Natansohn served in that capacity for six years before assuming the presidency in 1998. In 2000, when Orient was sold to Norwegian Cruise Line, she was

invited by Larry Pimentel and Pamela Conover to join Cunard in her present capacity.

Natansohn is frank to admit that the design and marketing of the *Queen Mary* project was without question "the most exciting and challenging effort of my career." She lived and breathed the vessel night and day, joined by a team of corporate colleagues responsible for every aspect of the new liner's on-board ambience "from choosing china patterns to planning the scope of entertainment." She relished the task of introducing a new generation of passengers to the delights of traditional yet vibrantly contemporary transatlantic travel.

Cunard's two top-ranked executives make an ideal team; Conover's financial expertise dovetails perfectly with Natansohn's marketing and sales strengths. Both women share a profound admiration not only for their company's hallowed past but their once-in-a-lifetime opportunity to create a remarkable Cunarder. "This was a company," muses Conover, "with fantastic brand equity." Restoring and burnishing that brand is a top priority. By the same token, Natansohn perceives herself firmly as "guardian of the incredible Cunard heritage."

In addition to port and starboard, every passenger vessel has two additional sides, the hotel and marine departments. Aboard *Queen Mary 2,* the hotel side is under the capable direction of Vice-President for Hotel Operations Lawrence Rapp. Thirty-eight years ago, Larry started with

Opposite: Barbara Broekman's tapestry portrait of *Queen Mary 2* in New York dominates the Brittania Restaurant. Appropriately, the captain's table is positioned directly beneath it. (© MICHEL VERDURE) *Above:* A sample of Cunard's provocative *haute couture* teaser ads, featuring models in splendid designer dresses dreaming about a voyage aboard *Queen Mary 2.*

Matson Line, followed by stints with American Hawaii and Pearl Cruises and Royal Viking Line. He was subsequently instrumental in the start-up of Seabourn Cruises. Larry oversees all QM2 hotel matters, including furnishings, food, drink, cabins, and entertainment.

His opposite number on the technical side, supervising all of *Queen Mary 2*'s formidable maritime requirements, is Milton Gonzales, Cunard's Vice-President of Marine & Technical Operations. A graduate of Duke University and the U.S. Merchant Marine Academy, Gonzales worked for fourteen years as director of Sea-Land Containers before coming aboard at Cunard. His present responsibilities include every detail of *QM2*'s marine and technical specifics, a cornucopia that includes safety, security, and port operations.

Another key person is Vice-President of Business Development Edie Bornstein. She is dauntingly articulate and enthusiastic, persuasive, and a master of the cold call. She has marshaled an exemplary collection of cultural institutions, chefs, and retailers into the tenor of *QM2* shipboard, prestigious components from both sides of the Atlantic. The moment a marketing or executive team came up with a co-branding inspiration, it was Bornstein who established contact and clinched the deal.

She was instrumental, for example, in bringing vintner Veuve Clicquot onboard, assigning its name permanently to the champagne bar and, significantly, to the bottle that christened the vessel. She also signed on two celebrated American chefs. Daniel Boulud—*wunderkind* of Manhattan's superb Daniel restaurant—was recruited as culinary adviser for the vessel's menus in the main restaurants. Prolific restaurateur Todd English was invited to set up his own shipboard restaurant at the after end of Deck 8. Bornstein followed up on Deborah Natansohn's brainstorm for RADA—London's famous Royal Academy of Dramatic Art—to create a shipboard theatrical repertory company, clinching the deal to bring on board rotating teams of actors and directors for top-notch theatrical performances. When the names Wedgwood and Waterford were bruited about, Bornstein convinced both firms to create a special pattern for the ship's two grills. (Britannia Restaurant's china adheres to Cunard's signature pattern, a traditional gold band adorned with a company logo.)

It was Enrichment Manager Mary Thomas who conceived the brilliant scheme that visiting academics from Oxford University's continuing education department should embark as a core Cunard ConneXions faculty, ensuring peerless academic input for passengers. And then there's the rose, a *Queen Mary 2* rose created especially by Meilland, the distinguished nursery in Provence. It is off-white, smells delicious, and is available on board. Veuve Clicquot, Daniel Boulud, Todd English, RADA, Oxford—the names speak for themselves.

With his naval architect's exterior a given, Micky Arison had next to assign the task of creating the vessel's interiors. For every shipboard designer, the *QM2* commission was enviable if for no other reason than that her towering air draft permitted public rooms of unprecedented height, verticality reminiscent of yesterday's vessels.

Arison's final decision was to divide the commission between two design entities; Sweden's Tillberg Design would be responsible for 80 percent of *QM2,* while design-team, a younger London firm, would handle the remainder.

Robert Tillberg was a designer new to Arison until a recently completed *QE2* renovation. Preeminent in his field, Tillberg is a tall, ruddy Swede with an enviable, forty-year maritime track record encompassing more than sixty passenger vessels. Starting his career as a painter, he went on to study furniture design. His maiden shipboard

venture was fitting out crew spaces aboard a cargo vessel. For one corner of a mess, Tillberg had ordered an ambitiously large corner sofa. As he and his fellow workers were struggling to shoehorn it into place, the owner joked that perhaps next time the young designer should let the yard know every sofa's size so they could build the vessel around his furniture!

It was a jest that would prove prescient. Robert Tillberg is perfectly attuned to the kind of upscale, distinguished finish that today's owners demand. His public rooms exhibit what a contemporary journalist has described as "luxuriant functionalism." Tillberg's expertise embraces not only furniture but also deckhouses and interiors, first with Baltic ferries and then fleets of world-class passenger ships, beginning with *Kungsholm* of 1966. Trailblazing *Sea Venture* and *Island Venture* followed. Since then, the Tillberg imprimatur has enriched an impressive roster of vessels, including some from Crystal Cruises, Norwegian Cruise Line, P&O, Royal Caribbean, Star Cruises, and, not surprisingly, Cunard; Tillberg renovated both *Sagafjord* and *Vistafjord* in the early nineties. Since his passenger vessel work had begun aboard Clyde-built *Kungsholm*, it pleases him that Cunard commissions for both *QE2* and *QM2* have brought him back, he reflects, "full circle:" *QE2*'s was the next keel section laid on John Brown's launch long after *Kungsholm*'s christening.

Tillberg Design boasts a worldwide presence. The head office is in Viken, a Swedish village near Helsingborg. The original structure has grown into a complex of generously windowed buildings, awash with light and free-flowing interiors. Members of his present-day design team work together in a new addition offering an offshore view of the Öresund, through which vessels they have designed periodically sail.

Opposite: Robert Tillberg pauses on one of the vessel's staircases, pleased with the successful completion of one of his most challenging commissions. *Above:* British artist Ian Cairnie, Art & Enterprise's head Erik Hermida, and SMC's Andy Collier deep in conference.

But these days, Tillberg is only a part-time Swedish resident. He lives currently in La Baule, convenient to nearby St.-Nazaire. Yet however remote from his native land, throughout Tillberg's oeuvre one detects haunting reminders of Viken's tranquil, midsummer northern light.

His oldest of four children, Tomas, heads up the firm's Fort Lauderdale office, which occupies most of a five-story, ship-shaped building. For designers with cruise ship aspirations, a meaningful Florida presence is mandatory. The convenient adjacency of Tillberg's Fort Lauderdale office to Carnival and Cunard in Miami ensured firsthand participation throughout the tentative initial design phase. Both Tillbergs, father and son, collaborated closely with Stephen Payne on the shape of the new Cunarder's provocative forward profile.

Tillberg's London headquarters is an English design firm called SMC. There, Andy Collier—a senior partner and "C" of the firm's triple-initial name—has been appointed project leader of the entire *Queen Mary 2* undertaking.

Tillberg's designated man for *Queen Mary 2* is Fredrik Johansson, a tall, genial Swede. He recounts that the Tillberg organization received the first "block form" GA on April 6, 1999, and only a (presumably frantic!) month later made a formal presentation to Micky Arison, Pamela Conover, and a Cunard team in Miami.

The other design firm hired for *QM2* was designteam, a successful company established only five years ago in London by partners Eric Mouzourides and Frank Symeou. Despite the firm's relatively brief existence, designteam has several important commissions under their collective belt, including work aboard Royal Caribbean's *Voyager*- and *Radiance*-class vessels as well as Celebrity's *Millennium*-class. They have also been designated lead designers for *Queen Victoria,* Cunard's latest newbuilding in Italy.

According to Mouzourides, his company's philosophy is a simple one: "We work hard and give our best. We are free-thinking, open-minded, and flexible." Suggests co-director Symeou, describing the firm's dedicated young design staff, "Everyone's opinion is valued, and pooling ideas often gives rise to some wonderful concepts." The partners strive to combine a high degree of professionalism—for which read *solid experience*—with innovative freshness.

The areas of responsibility designteam carried aboard *Queen Mary 2* include Illuminations, its surrounding Cunard Academy, Todd English's signature restaurant aft on Deck 8, as well as all Grand Lobby shops on Deck 3. The balance of the interiors—80 percent of the space—were created by Tillbert Design, including the Grand Lobby, Royal Court Theatre, Britannia Restaurant, Queens and Princess Grills, Commodore Club, the Queens Room, Canyon Ranch Spa Club®, and all cabins and staircases.

A Dutch company called Art & Enterprise was contracted to provide all of *QM2*'s works of art, a substantial collection valued at $5,000,000. This is the same firm that Holland America's Franz Dingerman has used to spectacular effect aboard many HAL newbuildings. From among their international stable of artists, Art & Enterprise has commissioned sculpture, bas-reliefs, tapestry, paintings, and prints—everything from major sculptural or woven pieces for the public rooms to hundreds of cabin and corridor lithographs.

Devised by a London company called The Open Agency is an in-depth, visual retrospective of Cunard history dubbed Maritime Quest. Informative wall panels containing text, photographs, paintings, and drawings document the company's transatlantic past. This heritage trail decorates the walls of all four staircases and also portions of Deck 7's promenades. Passengers can enjoy the entire series merely *en passant* or in more studious depth using a handheld, audio-guide device available at the Purser's Desk.

Now that we have met Cunard's brass and introduced the designers, what better time to explore the vessel itself, to examine the layout and logic of her interiors. In total, *Queen Mary 2* has seventeen decks stacked one atop another.

Two of them are ghost decks, because they do not exist as identifiable entities (read on). And the lowest four—double bottom, Deck B, Deck A, and Deck 1—do not, save with one exception, involve passengers.

The double bottom houses much of the ship's machinery. The vessel's crew are housed the length of Deck A and the forward part of Deck 1 just above it. They must descend one level for off-duty entertainment, to the Deck B pub, cinema, and gymnasium. Forward of the Deck B crew recreational complex is the ship's laundry, and aft a succession of capacious storerooms for every shipboard department—shops, library, hotel supplies, and uniforms.

Conversely, the crew ascends from their living quarters for meals, for the crew galley lies along Deck 1's port side amidships. Nearby are separate crew, staff, and officers' messes. There is another pub—Cunard crews' traditional Pig & Whistle—on the same deck.

Passengers bound for shore when *Queen Mary 2* is anchored out will descend as directed to one of Deck 1's four tender embarkation lounges. Each is assigned the name of a London district—Kensington, Belgravia, Knightsbridge, and Chelsea. Throughout sea days, these same passenger-friendly spaces will serve a multiplicity of uses. One, for example, becomes a card room, playing host to dozens of tables' worth of bridge addicts; aerobic classes will dominate another. Belgravia, forward on the port side, can double as supplementary waiting room for the ship's hospital while

Above: One of the delights of late-stage fitting out is witnessing the transformation of *QM2*'s public spaces to their final elegance. *Opposite:* Graceful, curving twin staircases join Decks 2 and 3 in *QM2*'s Grand Lobby. (© Michel Verdure)

Kensington—forward on the starboard side—will, of an evening, accommodate overflow of large cocktail parties held in the adjacent officers' wardroom. And, of course, at the start and end of crossings or cruises, passenger luggage is stacked to the ceiling of all four London lounges prior to disembarkation or, conversely, at the time of embarkation.

Given that Deck 1 is the supportive cellar, so to speak, of the main galley directly above it, nearly all its after end is devoted to provision and preparation rooms, the lowest link of the ship's long catering chain that extends upward through the hull. Throughout this lower-deck warren, consignments of meat, poultry, fish, and produce are retrieved from cold storage. Some must be thawed, others scrubbed, peeled, sliced, and diced; all are trundled onto elevators, destined for the galleys. We will discover, as we progress upward through *QM2*'s hull, that nearly all the ship's galleys are situated on a vertical path rising above this deck's preparation complex.

Next, we must ascend from crew territory into passenger country. One level higher, on Deck 2 amidships, *QM2*'s backstage metamorphoses dramatically into a fore stage. This is where the deadly serious business of *Queen Mary 2* begins. Save for bridge and engine room, no more crucial shipboard venue than a liner's threshold exists. Whether in New York or Southampton, it is through this maritime portal piercing the hull's shell plating that abiding first impressions are established.

Above: The Britannia Restaurant begins to take shape. *Opposite:* With tables set, the Britannia Restaurant awaits its first guests. (© MICHEL VERDURE)

Harried, flight-weary passengers, laden with hand luggage and sprung from the ennui of pier-side check-in, troop aboard their vessel, a moment anticipated for months. They are on board at last and *Queen Mary 2*'s unforgettable flavor is there for the tasting.

What do they find? They are welcomed into a sleek, glittering cosmos, lowest level of the Grand Lobby. This towering atrium, enriched with panoramic glass elevators, pierces upward through six decks. Ranged along Grand Lobby's starboard side is the hospitable crescent of the Purser's Desk, fount of welcome and problem-solving. Across the forward wall, Shore Excursion Desks await. Visible along the Grand Lobby's port side are the glittering lights and seductive electronic murmurs of the Empire Casino. The complimentary space to starboard is occupied by the cozy snuggery of Cunard's signature Golden Lion pub. These ancillary public spaces—purser's and Shorex desks, pub, and casino—surround the Grand Lobby's main embarkation level.

That this and the next level above it are connected by curving staircases underscores the architectural symbiosis uniting Decks 2 and 3. In fact, the two are conjoined by far more than numerical adjacency. Incorporated between Decks 2 and 3 is unseen but pivotal Deck 3L, the first of the two ghost decks mentioned above. This subtle, naval architectural legerdemain augments Deck 2's verticality, imparting monumental grandeur to its major public rooms. In fact, Decks 2, 3L, and 3 are united within one overwhelming cathedral of height for much of their length.

From where we stand in the Grand Lobby, we can turn left to go aft or right to go forward. Each direction will achieve one of shipboard's two overriding "E's"—eating and entertainment. Since passengers invariably dine before evening performances, let us proceed left into the vast reaches of the Britannia Restaurant. (Be aware that throughout the vessel, we will encounter public room names echoing prior nomenclature aboard *QE2*.)

This is *Queen Mary 2*'s main dining room, a stupendous modern-day counterpart of first Cunarder *Britannia*'s diminutive saloon of 1840. What an incredible contrast! The scale is sumptuous, the dimensions breathtaking. Since it must accommodate more than 1,300 passengers at a sitting,

the restaurant is composed of two hull-wide levels, the lower one on Deck 2 amplified by a commodious balcony level up on 3. Four behind-the-scenes escalators whisk stewards and their trays from Deck 2's galley up a flight to serve passengers assigned tables around the balcony.

For the record books, Payne has rewarded us with the first Cunarder in years to offer a double-tiered dining room. Not since *Lusitania*, *Mauretania,* or *Berengaria* have the company's passengers dined on more than one level. Aboard all three predecessor *Queen*s, restaurants of every class occupied one deck only.

Now Britannia Restaurant has effectively broken that mold, expanded to an exhilarating and festive height. It is one of the vessel's grandest spaces, satisfying every nuance of passenger showmanship. It can be entered either on Deck 2 as we have just done or, more dramatically, on its upper level. Indeed, at the Britannia's forward end, upper and lower levels are connected by twin, sinuously curving staircases lined with clear glass railings, tailor-made for languid, ceremonial descents.

The tables and their surrounding paneled walls are illuminated from three sources—pin-point spotlights, a huge recessed illuminated ceiling coffer, and a series of tulip-shaped, onyx urns. Towering classical columns rear up to either side, supporting the pale gray ceiling.

After dinner, we can leave both levels of the Britannia Restaurant either forward or aft. In either direction, evening entertainment awaits. Exiting aft from the restaurant's upper level, proceed with me across an after staircase lobby into the Queens Room, as on *QE2,* a venue for music, dancing, and occasional cabaret.

Unlike any other of the Decks 2 and 3 public rooms, the Queens Room boasts only one level, sited directly atop the galley. That single deck height notwithstanding, the space is impressive, incorporating as it does a large, recessed ceiling. Tillberg has created a splendidly traditional facility that instantly summons to mind *Berengaria*'s lavish B-Deck ballroom. Underfoot is a huge, inlaid dance floor—the largest afloat—and overhead a glittering crystal chandelier. Surrounding tables and chairs accommodate dancers between sets. The bandstand is sited along the room's after wall, framed prettily within an art deco, half-round proscenium. In addition to offering nightly dancing and cabaret, the Queens Room is where passengers will each be photographed with the captain, a time-honored Cunard ritual known fleet-wide as "the captain's handshake."

Conversely, if we exit forward from Britannia Restaurant's upper level, we meander towards the bow—as countless passengers will after dinner—en route to shows just the other side of the Grand Lobby. Deck 3's level surrounding the Grand Lobby is bar country—no less than three separate watering spots invite our attendance before and after meals. To starboard we pass another

Above: Along with the Queens Grill, the Princess Grill offers exquisite dining on an intimate scale. (© MICHEL VERDURE) *Opposite*: Resplendent with its half-round proscenium, twin chandeliers, and the vessel's full width, the Queens Room is the largest and handsomest ballroom afloat. (© MICHEL VERDURE)

QE2 legacy, the Chart Room. Hard by it, with a view overlooking the atrium, is the Veuve Clicquot Champagne Bar. Over on the port side is Sir Samuel's Wine Bar.

The remaining quadrants around the Grand Lobby on Deck 3 are given over to suites of Mayfair shops where clothing, souvenirs, jewelry, perfume, books, and sundries are on inviting display at this busy passenger crossroad.

Resisting the urge to browse or buy, we press forward, via the ship's central thoroughfare, past a bank of six midship elevators toward the first of *Queen Mary 2*'s two great entertainment facilities, one sited directly beyond the other. This consecutive nesting, so to speak, of two major auditoria is one of Stephen Payne's inspired shipboard provisions.

Nearest and first is the Royal Court Theatre, named after London's Sloane Square original. This is an extremely ambitious and well-equipped show lounge. We have entered the auditorium at balcony level, overlooking a generous orchestra floor spread out below on Deck 2. An audience of just over 1,100 can be accommodated in ascending crescents of seats.

Incorporated within the Theatre is an arsenal of sophisticated stage machinery the Sloane Square original might well envy. Within its proscenium arch, the stage not only revolves, but is divided into four athwartship platforms, each one of which can be elevated by remote command to varying heights. Another roving platform is situated at the bottom of the orchestra pit. If required, a show band playing in the pit can rise magically on cue to orchestra floor level before proceeding upstage as far as the back wall. This is the kind of stunning scenic effect pioneered

Opposite: Illumination's planetarium dome is rigged for viewing, shown here lowered from its stored position within the ceiling. *Above:* A glorious expanse of celestial geography appears as if by magic within the finished dome.

in New York's Radio City Music Hall and seldom experienced afloat.

More magic is concealed overhead. A capacious fly floor stores flats and fiber-optical drops out of sight. And the Theatre's final scenic ace-in-the-hole is a stage-wide video wall that can be flown in and out on demand.

Show biz riches continue forward. Situated immediately beyond the Royal Court Theatre—tucked in behind its capacious backstage—is another, smaller amphitheater, christened Illuminations. The triple-threat space created by designteam fulfills several multimedia roles as cinema, lecture hall, and—a first aboard any vessel anywhere—a working planetarium. Although vibration is unlikely that far forward or deep within the hull, six "Sky-Cam" projectors have been installed permanently amongst audience rows, allowing projection up to an overhead dome that can be lowered into place within minutes. Far out at sea, Illuminations can conjure up peerless celestial displays or programs fully the equal of those mounted within shoreside planetaria in both London and New York. The seats are steeply raked, and wrapped around a stage buttressed with three enhancing video screens.

Within a state-of-the-art projection booth, twin 35-millimeter projectors guarantee a contemporary shipboard rarity: superb film screenings. Already a unique plus aboard *Queen Elizabeth 2*, in these days of inferior videotaped movies shown elsewhere, first-class theatrical projection continues gloriously aboard *Queen Mary 2*.

The close contiguity of these two auditoria, one located directly ahead of the other, necessitated some last-minute GA refinement. Once again, in-house expertise was conveniently at hand. Micky Arison asked Joe Farcus, his resident interior architect, to help ease several vexing flow problems: how best to achieve either one of *QM2*'s performance venues without neglecting the other and, even more important, without confusing passengers.

Suggests Farcus, "The big trap for architects is we tend to think big . . . When you're working on deck plans, you're a giant. But you can't forget that people don't see it that way; they're not five hundred feet up in the air. You have to think big initially and then think small to work out the final details."

A man with fine-tuned antennae about assisting passengers through complex deck schemes, Joe recommended shrinking the Royal Court Theatre's lateral dimension sufficiently to permit provision of flanking promenades. Readily accessible and identifiable from the Theatre's lobby, these vital detours invite those bound for movie rather than show to bypass the Theatre and continue forward to Illuminations.

En route, they will find yet a third entertainment option, another *QM2* novelty. Anticipating the lobby of Illuminations is ConneXions, a spread of seven sizable "classrooms" devoted to interactive passenger instruction. Dubbed the Cunard Academy, here is shipboard enrichment in the truest sense, learning and/or communication imparted by University of Oxford faculty and a generous array of computer consoles. Within this floating academia, expandable spaces offer specialized talks and seminars to passenger participants on a wide variety of subjects. If desired, any college room presentation can be electronically projected onto the Illuminations big screen.

Farcus must be given credit for some additional GA refinements, one of them a provision of Grand Lobby's towering atrium. During the original design phase, former Cunard president Larry Pimentel felt that an atrium was unnecessary. But as Farcus confided, the Arison/Farcus consensus was that passengers would expect one. Aft of that now Grand(er) Lobby, the challenge of bypassing the Royal Court Theatre to achieve Illuminations is repeated toward the stern where the Britannia Restaurant interfaces with the Queens Room. Farcus recommended creation of what he describes as "mini-atriums" to facilitate entry into the Queens Room along both Decks 2 and 3. And once more, thanks to ghost Deck L3, two flanking promenades—the same kind that access Illuminations—circumvent the Britannia's lower level. The starboard one houses Images, the vessel's photographic venue, while on the opposite side of the vessel the ship's art gallery occupies the fore-and-aft connector.

Final destination thanks to Deck 3L is the vessel's diminutive, late-night hideaway, the G32 disco, named after this fourth *Queen*'s St.-Nazaire hull number and

reminiscent of the Q4 club on *QE2*'s original deck plan. Here, nightowls will congregate into the small hours. Since it is a completely interior space, every afternoon teenagers will gather either for dancing or every adolescent's inevitable preference, hanging out.

Our horizontal walkabout throughout Decks 2, 3L, and 3 concluded, let us ascend. The next three levels up—Decks 4, 5, and 6—are devoted almost exclusively to passenger cabins, most with balconies sculpted out of the hull. The sole exception is a complex for *Queen Mary 2*'s younger cruisers located on the after end of Deck 6. Indoors, children of all ages are welcomed into either a nursery staffed by trained nannies or playrooms full of games, toys, and all those electronic gadgets that often

Above: Dutch artist Harald Vlgut's *The Signs of Seeing* uses Einstein's face and a double helix to embody ConneXion's quest for knowledge. *Opposite:* Just aft of the Queens room is the G32 room, named after *QM2*'s shipyard monicker. A mechanistic dream, it caters to teenagers by day and adults by night. (© MICHEL VERDURE)

only young minds and hands can master. Outdoors, looking over the stern, is a children's swimming area, with a small splash pool forward and, though a larger body of water, what deck plans still describe as the Minnows pool.

We emerge on Deck 7 (topmost stop for the Grand Lobby's panoramic elevators) to encounter the vessel's third great public-room deck. This level of *Queen Mary 2* also incorporates the second of Stephen Payne's ghost decks, identified on his plan simply as "Open 'Tween Deck." Though it amplifies Deck 7's ceiling height, the naval architectural rationale here is less for grandeur than safety; vertical expansion is essential to accommodate lifeboat rows suspended above both flanking exteriors.

Indeed, were Deck 7 to be assigned a generic name, it would surely be Promenade Deck, as an inviting quarter-mile of teak enwraps the entire deckhouse. A protected interior crossover circles the bow and beyond it lies a forward-facing observation deck.

After one exploratory circumnavigation, let us retrace our steps to explore Deck 7's forward interior. Immediately, we are engulfed within an epicurean complex dedicated to a paradoxical combination of self-improvement and self-indulgence. Whereas Decks 2 and 3 infuse passenger minds and bodies with gastronomic, amusement, and intellectual sustenance, up here those minds and bodies are kept in sound emotional and physical trim.

Occupying all of Deck 7's forward end lies the hushed, luxurious surround of Canyon Ranch SpaClub, *Queen Mary 2*'s state-of-the-art wellness center. Since Canyon Ranch remains incontrovertibly the most *recherché* spa in the United States, finding one established aboard *QM2* represents an incredible passenger plus.

This is the world's fourth Canyon Ranch spa, a floating replication of land-based prototypes in Arizona, the Berkshires, and Las Vegas's Venetian Hotel. It is a lavish facility that promotes therapy rather than mere products. A gymnasium and weight rooms share the view over the bow and, just aft, within two dozen treatment rooms, a cadre of experienced Canyon Ranch personnel offers a healthful and rejuvenating cornucopia—massages and body work, mud, aromatherapy, ayurvedic and seaweed treatments, facials and masks, wraps and body scrubs. Sixty

different thalassotherapy treatments are available in a central pool, and in the adjacent thermal suite are aromatic steam rooms, as well as herbal and Finnish saunas.

Aft, adhering to the deckhouse's starboard side, is the Winter Garden, its extravagantly foliated *faux* skylight and lavish plantings a heartening update of garden lounges aboard *Aquitania* and the first two *Queens*. This wicker-furnished retreat is a perfect venue for tea. It is also a space for quiet reading, companionable chatting, knitting and needlepointing, a game of patience, or succumbing to that ubiquitous midocean temptation, postprandial dozing.

Leaving the Winter Garden, the way aft lies along an off-center corridor. Gastronomy reigns the balance of Deck 7. We enter first into the King's Court, the vessel's lido, to use the generic term. Suiting *QM2*'s transatlantic stance, it has no outdoor access, but to either side five windowed bays compensate nicely by extending the interior out into flanking promenades.

Housed within its capacious length are several intriguing catering alternatives. There was a time when shipboard lidos offered only buffet breakfast and lunch, thereafter slumbering deserted until the following morning. No more: At dusk, Kings Court is transformed into four contrasting restaurants. Once ingenious partitions have been deployed, different illumination, china and waiters' uniforms arranged, formerly disparate art and mosaics surrounding the daytime buffet area assume their rightful decorative

Opposite: The lavish thalassotherapy pool in the Canyon Ranch Spa has a replica of a huge snail shell perched on its teak surround. (© MICHEL VERDURE) *Above*: A view of the Winter Garden's wicker furniture with Ian Cairnie's palm-foliated conservatory ceiling above it. (© MICHEL VERDURE)

contiguity. Reserving tables through a central reservation number, passengers can dine in either the oriental Lotus, the British Carvery, with a Continental twist, *trattoria* La Piazza, or, perhaps most intriguing, the innovative Chef's Galley. In the latter, thirty-five lucky diners will watch that evening's dinner-to-come being prepared, gratifying passengers' insatiable curiosities about shipboard food, its consumption no less than its preparation.

At the after end of Deck 7 are two more dining rooms, reappearances of familiar, upscale *QE2* originals, Queens Grill to starboard—complete with its own designated cocktail lounge—and Princess Grill to port, each with superb ocean views across the surrounding promenade. Here occupants of the ship's most expensive accommodations will breakfast, lunch, and dine at extended-hour sittings. Meals for both grills are prepared within a single, dedicated galley.

Up a level, overlooking a swimming terrace spanning the after end of Deck 8, is another restaurant given the name of the American chef whose culinary inspiration defines it, Todd English. Diners will face aft through an athwartship span of glass, an identical venue to the first *Queen Mary's* fondly recalled Veranda Grill.

As long as we are at the stern, it is worth climbing higher. Directly above Todd English's establishment, Decks 9 and 10 are devoted exclusively to suites and cabins. But adorning Deck 11's after end is a private outdoor aerie for the exclusive use of Queens Grill passengers, the only class-restricted deck on board, complete with its own hot tub and bar.

Two decks higher, passengers once more emerge outdoors into the vessel's upper-deck sports complex, a breathtaking two hundred feet (sixty-one meters) above the sea. At the stern are dog kennels and the Boardwalk Café, haven for the fast food lunches that swimmers in damp bathing suits crave. Just forward of the funnel's embrace is a swimming pool, protected when necessary by a retractable glass roof. Forward of that, up a flight of steps, is a vast open sun-bowl with another pool, surrounded by golf-driving simulators, paddle and table-tennis courts and an indoor sports center and the Lookout.

Last on our inspection tour are the vessel's forward-facing interiors. By descending to Deck 7 and proceeding forward to the Canyon Ranch SpaClub, we can reascend using one of the exterior panoramic elevators tucked behind the bridge. Their vertical itinerary begins on Deck 7 and either one will carry us up to every public (and private) room sited within the bridge screen's generous arc.

But before we embark in our delightfully scenic conveyance, a lightning primer about the ship's geography. Dual coordinates—horizontal decks and vertical stairwells—are mandatory aboard every passenger vessel. *Queen Mary 2* has four staircases spread the length of the vessel, lettered A, B, C, and D from bow to stern. Of course, each stairwell incorporates elevators as well. Although only three elevator cars serve less-used A and D, six—two facing banks of three each—respond to more heavily trafficked B and C staircases near the vessel's center.

Now, slip into the starboard side's panoramic elevator. Pushing the button for Deck 8, we are lofted upward one level to emerge into the ship's combined library and writing room. Connected directly aft of this space is the splendid book shop managed by Ocean Books, duplication of that extremely popular passenger destination aboard *QE2*. On the port side of this deck is the beauty salon, venue for hairdressing and manicure, a vertical extension of Canyon Ranch SpaClub, achieved from Deck 7 either by interior staircase or, more effortlessly and scenically, via the portside's panoramic elevator.

Back to our vertical quest. One level higher, we enter within the great span of glass enclosing the Commodore Club, Deck 9's only public room and also the only forward interior save the wheelhouse that encompasses the entire bridge screen. This is a splendid panoramic bar overlooking the bow, an absolute must for cocktails before lunch and dinner or entry into port. Ancillary space aft includes the Board Room to port for private meetings and, on the starboard side, the Cigar Lounge, a cozy retreat for the vessel's Havana connoisseurs and a last vestige of former Cunarders' traditional smoking rooms.

We resume our vertical tour to find that since Deck 10 is VIP country only, stopping there requires a special passkey. The sweep of bridge screen glass has been segmented

Opposite: The interior of the Todd English Restaurant aft on Deck 8. (© Michel Verdure)

tion deck, enclosing at its center an interior space for meetings, perfectly named the Atlantic Room.

Had we been able to float upward one more level, we would have reached the bridge. This ultimate command center incorporates wheelhouse, chartroom, safety center, and master's and staff captain's quarters. Unlike many contemporary cruise ships, no passenger lounge is sited above it. During an early design phase, former president Larry Pimentel suggested to Stephen Payne that he incorporate such a feature, but traditionalist Payne demurred and talked him out of it. No Cunarder has ever had a public room atop the bridge and he was not anxious to create a precedent aboard *QM2*.

A vessel's bridge is not only its visual pinnacle, it serves as figurative summit as well. Having it topped by a lounge somehow demeans that maritime sovereignty. So the convex dome surmounting *QM2*'s bridge houses air conditioning machinery and elevator hoists only.

Our arrival at the bridge not only completes our *QM2* walkabout but also serves as an apropos moment to introduce the master. Commodore Ron Warwick has been a familiar host to *QE2* passengers for years; what better capstone to his long career than continuing that role aboard the company's latest flagship?

Born into a seafaring family, Commodore Warwick's merchant navy career began at the age of fifteen aboard training ship HMS *Conway* on North Wales. His first years of indentured apprenticeship were with the Port Line, trading cargo out to Australia and New Zealand. Awarded his second mate's certificate in 1961, he worked on several cargo vessels, experiencing life aboard a wide variety of ships. But it was a pivotal tour of duty as fourth officer aboard Royal Mail Line's *Andes* in the mid-sixties that, fortuitously for us, convinced the young officer that passenger ships lay undeniably in his future.

Steady promotion continued. Chief Officer Ron Warwick served aboard another cargo vessel in 1967 and obtained his master's ticket the following year. In 1971, he signed on with Cunard Line, appointed junior officer aboard *Carmania*. Assignments aboard a flotilla of Cunarders followed, including *QE2*, *Cunard Adventurer*, *Cunard Countess*, *Cunard Princess*, and *Crown Dynasty*. Finally,

again, offering incomparable forward views for four huge staterooms. I christen them collectively "the Queen suites," each one boasting up to 1,194 square feet (998 square meters) of unparalleled shipboard luxe high above the bow. Only legitimate occupants or expected guests can enter. The starboard side's Queen Elizabeth suite has as its mirrored equivalent to port the Queen Mary suite. The two central accommodations—Queen Anne port of the keel line and Queen Victoria starboard—are achieved using the A Staircase.

After tiptoeing out, we rise to Deck 11, the end of this elevator line. Here we can enjoy a splendid open observa-

Opposite: Under way at full speed, *Queen Mary 2* performs well on her builder's trials. *Above*: Commodore Ron Warwick on the bridge of *QM2*. He received this appointment shortly before *QM2*'s christening.

in 1986, he assumed his first command aboard *Cunard Princess* in Alaskan waters.

Commodore Warwick is the author of a definitive history of *Queen Elizabeth 2*, published by Norton. Additionally, his all-consuming—and, for maritime historians, extremely useful—hobby is the creation of an exhaustive data base listing the names, dates, and careers of every Cunard master since the company's founding in 1839.

The timing of his initial Cunard tour back in 1971 is important. Two years previous had seen the debut of *Queen Elizabeth 2*. Sailing in command of that innovative third *Queen* was none other than Ron's father, Captain Bil Warwick—not William, not Bill, but decisively Bil. A genial and beloved master, Bil Warwick founded, in effect, a remarkable shipboard dynasty. Bearded Warwick senior retired from *QE2* in 1972; eighteen years later, bearded Warwick junior became *QE2*'s master.

It was a remarkable succession. In the annals of merchant shipping history, no father and son have ever commanded the same ocean liner. Ron's appointment coincided with the auspicious visit of Her Majesty Queen Elizabeth and His Royal Highness Prince Philip aboard the flagship to celebrate the occasion of Cunard's sesquicentennial at Spithead in July 1990.

Unquestionably, the crowning achievement of Commodore Warwick's career was being selected master-designate of this ultimate Cunarder. Normally, a captain destined for important promotion is summoned to company headquarters, but in this event the mountain came to Mohammed.

It was March 1998, near the end of *QE2*'s world cruise; then-President Larry Pimentel and COO Pamela Conover flew to Cape Town for an onboard meeting with Captain Warwick. There, they asked him if he would be willing to delay his retirement to bring out the new ship.

"As you can imagine," Ron wrote me some years later," it was a great honor just to be asked. The only person I told was my wife Kim. I didn't even mention it to my father before he died." That failure to share the monumental news with Bil Warwick before his sudden and unexpected death troubles his son, knowing how thrilled the old man would have been. At the same time, Captain Paul Wright was designated relief master

On March 13, 2003, with his new ship's hull already afloat in St.-Nazaire, Captain and Mrs. Warwick disembarked from *Queen Elizabeth 2* for the last time at Kobe, in the midst of her 2003 world cruise. He shared details of final chores aboard their beloved vessel: "Kim blew the whistle and I painted the funnel."

Now, let us take temporary leave of Ron Warwick and his exciting new command, relinquishing modern-day Cunard for company history. We must return to the early nineteenth century and document the genesis of this durable North Atlantic institution.

Above: Behind the generous sweep of the bar in the Commodore Club, Henk Brandwijk's superb model of *Queen Mary 2* is encased in glass. (© MICHEL VERDURE) *Opposite:* Twinned black uprights towering in the Grand Lobby each support a panoramic elevator rising up to Deck 7. *Overleaf:* Commodore Ron Warwick in command on his bridge.

Opposite: The view aft from the bridge, showing the starboard side's long sweep of balconied cabins extending into the distance. Poised just above Deck 7's promenade is that reassuring sentinel row of lifeboats. *Above:* The lower level of the elaborate Balmoral Suite. (© Michel Verdure) *Overleaf:* Along the corridor aft of the Grand Lobby is one of four scenic bas-reliefs by Gonzales & Harms.

Opposite: A mosaic-floored ante room in Kings Court. To the left, Chef's Galley; to the right, La Piazza Italian Restaurant. *Above*: The Play Zone offers a colorful retreat of learning and creativity for *QM2*'s youngest passengers. (© MICHEL VERDURE) *Overleaf: Queen Mary 2* lies at rest, bathed in late afternoon light; Stephen Payne's formidable bow structure accentuates the hull's long grace.

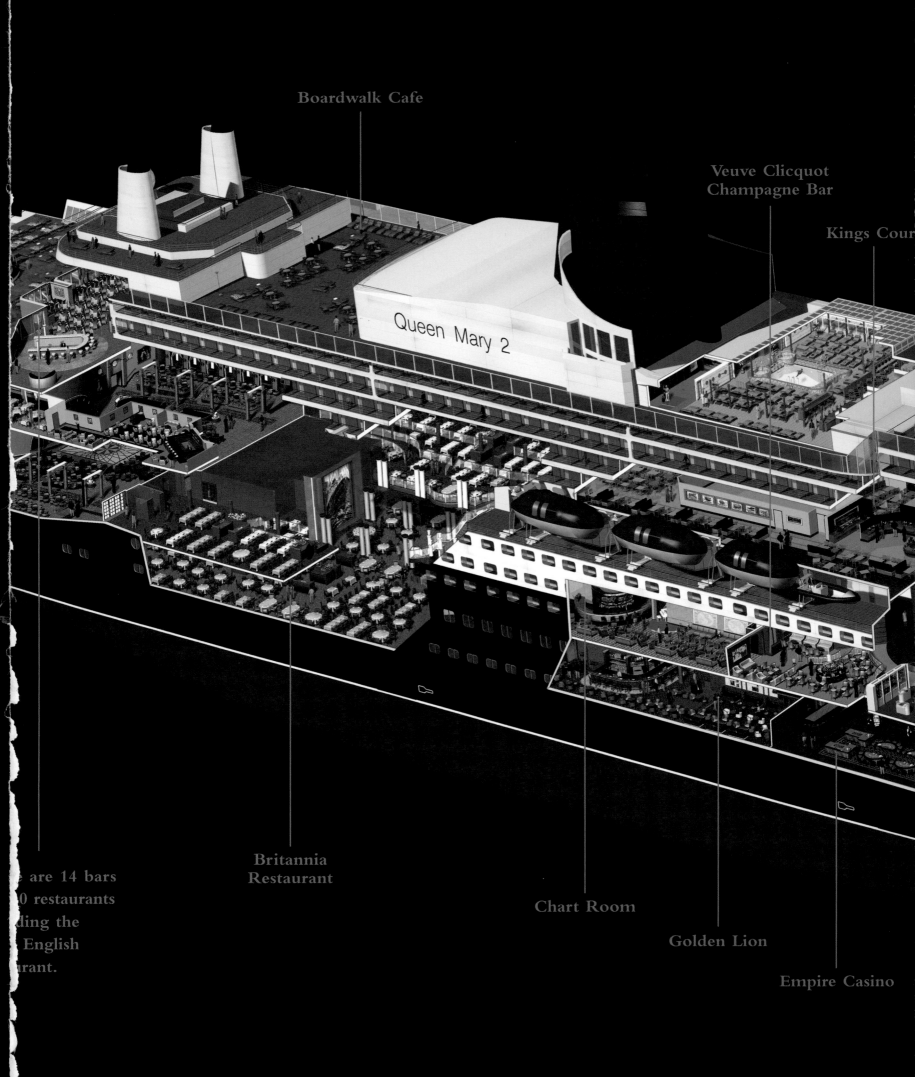

Boardwalk Cafe

Veuve Clicquot
Champagne Bar

Kings Cour

Queen Mary 2

Britannia
Restaurant

are 14 bars
0 restaurants
ding the
English
urant.

Chart Room

Golden Lion

Empire Casino

Length: 1132 feet
Beam: 135 feet
Beam at Bridge Wings: 164 feet
Draft: 32.8 feet
Height (Keel to Funnel): 236.2 feet
Gross Registered Tonnage: Approximately 150,000 tons
Passengers: 2620
Crew: 1254
Top Speed: Approximately 30 knots (34.5 mph)

Power: 157,000 horsepower
Environmentally friendly, gas turbine/diesel electric plant
Propulsion: Four pods of 21.5 MW each: 2 fixed and 2 azimuthing
Strength: Extra thick steel hull for strength and stability for Atlantic trade
Stabilizers: Two sets
Cost: 780 million dollars

Some comparisons:

QM2 is five times longer than Cunard's first ship, Britannia (230 ft.)
QM2 is more than twice as long as the Washington Monument is tall (550 ft.)
QM2 is 147 feet longer than the Eiffel Tower is tall (984 ft.)
QM2 is more than 3.5 times as long as Westminster Tower (Big Ben) is high (310 ft.)
QM2 is only 117 feet shorter than the Empire State Building is tall (1248 ft.)
QM2 is more than three times as long as St. Paul's Cathedral is tall (366 ft.)
QM2 is as long as 36 double-decker London buses (31.5 ft. each)
QM2's whistle will be audible for ten miles.

Queens Grill

Queens Room

G32
Nightclub

Th
and
inc
Toc
rest

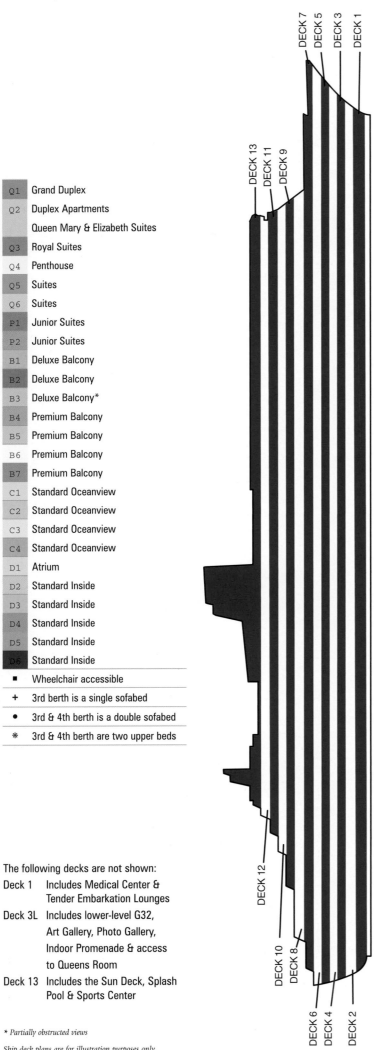

Q1	Grand Duplex
Q2	Duplex Apartments
	Queen Mary & Elizabeth Suites
Q3	Royal Suites
Q4	Penthouse
Q5	Suites
Q6	Suites
P1	Junior Suites
P2	Junior Suites
B1	Deluxe Balcony
B2	Deluxe Balcony
B3	Deluxe Balcony*
B4	Premium Balcony
B5	Premium Balcony
B6	Premium Balcony
B7	Premium Balcony
C1	Standard Oceanview
C2	Standard Oceanview
C3	Standard Oceanview
C4	Standard Oceanview
D1	Atrium
D2	Standard Inside
D3	Standard Inside
D4	Standard Inside
D5	Standard Inside
D6	Standard Inside
■	Wheelchair accessible
+	3rd berth is a single sofabed
●	3rd & 4th berth is a double sofabed
✳	3rd & 4th berth are two upper beds

The following decks are not shown:

Deck 1 — Includes Medical Center & Tender Embarkation Lounges

Deck 3L — Includes lower-level G32, Art Gallery, Photo Gallery, Indoor Promenade & access to Queens Room

Deck 13 — Includes the Sun Deck, Splash Pool & Sports Center

Partially obstructed views

Ship deck plans are for illustration purposes only. Actual cabins may vary, decks are not to scale.

Deck 13   Deck 12   Deck 11

Deck 10

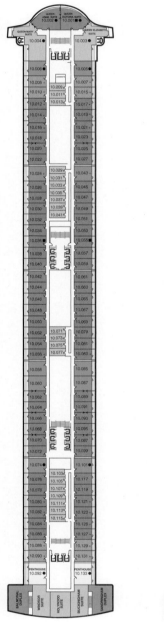

Deck 9

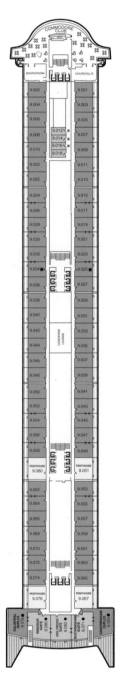

Deck 8

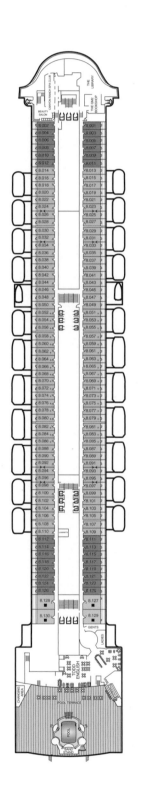

Deck 7

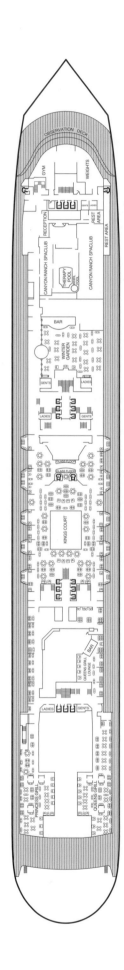

Deck 6

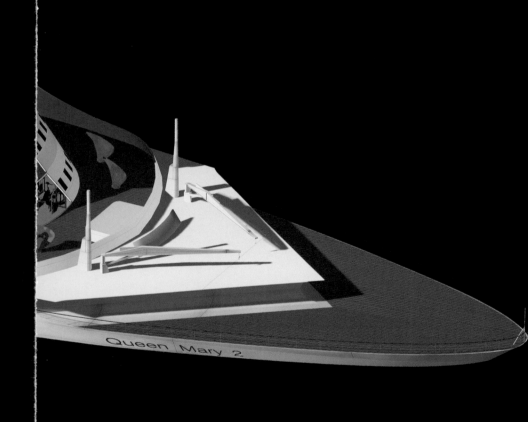
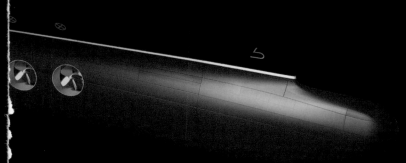

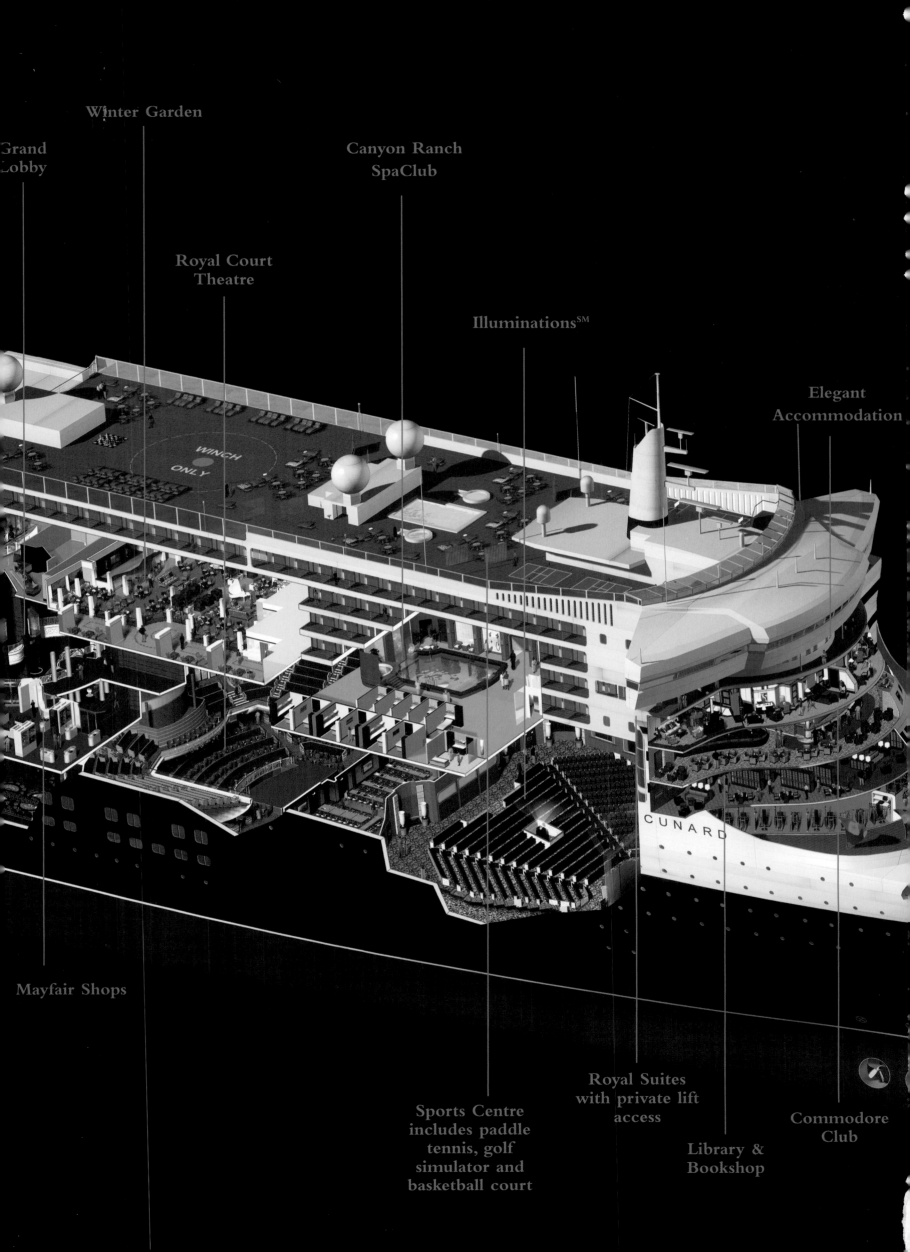

Winter Garden

Grand
Lobby

Canyon Ranch
SpaClub

Royal Court
Theatre

Illuminations^{SM}

Elegant
Accommodation

WINCH
ONLY

CUNARD

Mayfair Shops

Royal Suites
with private lift
access

Sports Centre
includes paddle
tennis, golf
simulator and
basketball court

Library &
Bookshop

Commodore
Club

Deck 5

Deck 4

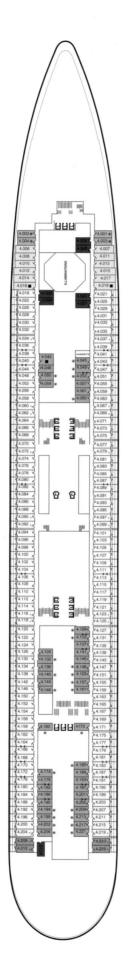

Deck 3

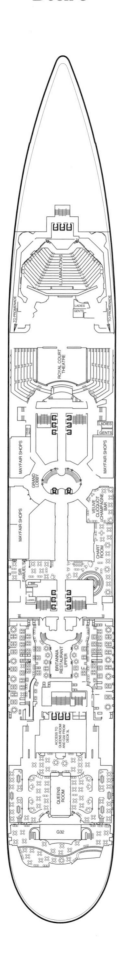

Deck 2

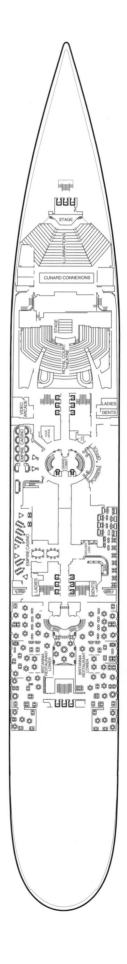

Sir Samuel's Novel Service

From Halifax came Joe Cunard
His father worked in the Navy Yard;
But his brother Sam made the neighbors stare
They said he would be a millionaire.

—Anonymous Halifax doggerel

Samuel Cunard's unassailable niche in mercantile history is assured forever. The shipping line he founded in 1840 revolutionized transatlantic passenger life, the first steamship service connecting Great Britain with North America.

The word "service" is significant. Deployment of four transatlantic paddle wheelers within seven months was an unprecedented feat. These were not one-of-a-kind, experimental steamships but a fleet of identical packets. From 1840 on, a Cunarder sailed westbound every fortnight delivering Royal Mail to North America.

Although the Cunards became Canadian by choice, their forebears were descendants of German Quakers who settled in Pennsylvania's Germantown in 1683. Samuel's great-great grandfather was Thones Kunder. (The family name metamorphosed from Kunder to Conrad to Cunrad and finally to Cunard.) Thones's great-grandson Abraham established a successful shipping company. But when the colonies declared their independence, staunch loyalist Abraham Cunard's fleet and warehouses were confiscated. Ruined, he fled to Canada.

Halifax was a haven for exiles abandoning the rebellious colonies. Reduced from shipowner to laborer, Abraham Cunard worked as a carpenter at Halifax's Royal Naval Dockyard. He married fellow loyalist Margaret Murphy, a Roman Catholic exiled from South Carolina.

Their second son, Samuel, was born on November 21, 1787, middle sibling between Joseph and Henry. Samuel attended Halifax Grammar School and proved an astute young entrepreneur. He would buy damaged coffee and spice shipments at auction, wrap the residue into little packets and peddle them door-to-door.

After working in the engineering department of a Halifax lumberyard, Samuel went to Boston apprenticed to a ship broker. Three years later he returned to Halifax, age twenty-one, to work for newly established Abraham Cunard & Son. The firm prospered, thanks to a welcome infusion of capital realized from a prize ship. While brothers

Joseph and Henry served aboard company tonnage as sailors, Samuel remained at headquarters.

In 1814, he and his father established a mail service between Halifax, Boston, Newfoundland, and Bermuda. That same year, Samuel married Susan Duffus, who bore him two sons and seven daughters before leaving him a widower ten years later. The firm of A. Cunard & Son fielded a growing fleet, among them the *Margaret*, the *Nancy*, and the *White Oak*. The latter had crossed to England in 1813, Cunard's first transatlantic vessel.

Shortly after his favorite son's marriage, Abraham Cunard relinquished control of A. Cunard & Son to Samuel, and A. Cunard & Son reverted simply to S. Cunard. By 1827, at the age of forty, Samuel was an influential and highly respected millionaire.

What kind of figure did Samuel Cunard cut? "A bright little man with keen eyes, firm lips, and happy manners, somewhat below middle height," reported one observer. He was described by a fellow Haligonian as "vigorous in frame with exceptional nerve force and great powers of endurance; brisk of step, brimful of energy and always on the alert."

The burgeoning possibilities of a steamship service intrigued him. In 1833, he was one of 144 subscribers who underwrote construction of paddle steamer *Royal William*. She crossed to Britain in a respectable seventeen days, surpassing older, less adventurous rivals. America's Black Ball, Dramatic, and Shakespeare Lines preferred to crowd on every possible sail, remaining loyal to canvas rather than newfangled steam.

Throughout the mid-1830s, Cunard's forty-ship fleet distributed the Royal Mail that, dispatched from Falmouth on England's south coast, docked six weeks later at King's Wharf in Halifax. The laggardly performance of these superannuated, ten-gun brigs galled Samuel Cunard. Inspired by *Royal William*'s success, he wanted to supplant the Admiralty's archaic mail ships with something more up-to-date.

Overleaf: Along first *Queen Elizabeth*'s Sports Deck, bundled up passengers enjoy some bracing, midocean air. *Above:* Sir Samuel Cunard, the man who revolutionized transatlantic passenger service. *Opposite: Britannia* crossed in the summer of 1840, the first of dozens of Cunarders to follow.

He was not alone. In 1838, the lord commissioner of the Admiralty solicited tenders for a steam service to carry the North American mails. The seven-year contract would oblige successful candidates to dispatch a mail ship every fortnight between Liverpool, Halifax, and Boston in return for an annual subsidy of £55,000.

No American shipping line responded and only two rival British companies did. Obtaining no support from either Boston or Halifax investors, Cunard crossed immediately to Britain. There, in short order, he raised £270,000 from a trio of Scots—David McIver, George Burns, and Robert Napier. The first two were shipping men while Napier was, fortuitously, a Glaswegian shipbuilder.

The enterprise boasted thirty-three partners in all, with Samuel Cunard as the largest investor. Their selected company name said it all—The British & North American Royal Mail Steam Packet Company; passengers called it simply "the Cunard Line."

George Burns supervised ship construction while McIver established a Liverpool terminus. First of the class Britannia, built by Robert Duncan of Greenock, was launched on February 5, 1840. Displacing 1,140 tons, she was 200 feet (61 meters) overall with a 32-foot (9.75-meter) beam. She was rigged as a three-masted barque and could accommodate 115 passengers.

Two side-lever engines were installed amidships, 70-inch cylinders with 6-foot (2-meter) stroke, driven by steam at 9 pounds per square inch, producing 420 horsepower. Twenty-eight foot (8.5 meters) diameter paddle wheels revolved sixteen times a minute. Daily coal consumption was 40 tons, mandating bunkers accommodating 640 tons.

Cunard planned originally for three steamers but Napier urged addition of a fourth; the Admiralty increased their subsidy by £5,000 *per annum*. Sistership *Acadia* entered service a month after *Britannia,* on August 4, 1840. *Caledonia* first sailed September 19, and the fourth, *Columbia,* embarked her first passengers on January 5, 1841.

A Cunarder steamed out of Liverpool on the fourth and nineteenth of every month except during November, December, January, and February, when they sailed only on the fourth. Of the four, *Acadia* was the most successful, holding the Blue Ribband for five years.

After one year, Cunard found his costs too high and obtained a second subsidy increase to £81,000, on the condition that a fifth steamer be added. She was *Hibernia,* eight feet longer than her fleet-mates and accommodating 120 passengers rather than 115.

Cunard's enthusiasm was coupled with exemplary thoroughness. He signed the mail contract, built and manned his first vessel, and achieved its maiden voyage within sixteen months, an enviable achievement. Although he ordained ships and crews of the first rank—"nothing but the best ships, the best officers and the best men"— a bedrock of stubborn, Haligonian practicality lay beneath.

Above: Shown here in its glass case aboard *Queen Elizabeth 2,* the Boston Cup has been transferred to replacement flagship *Queen Mary 2.*

*Steamers properly built and manned might start
and arrive at their destination with the punctuality
of railway trains on land...We have no tunnels to drive,
no cuttings to make, no roadbeds to prepare. We need
only build our ships and start them to work.*

—Samuel Cunard

Shipbuilders were advised, "I want a plain and comfortable boat, not the least unnecessary expense for show." All five vessels' names ended with the letters "-ia," establishing a consistent naming policy for nearly a century.

Britannia sailed from Liverpool on July 4, 1840, a patriotic date not lost on his American clientele. The sixty-three passengers embarked included the founder and one of his daughters. In command of ninety crewmen was Captain Henry Woodruff, R.N. The final cargo loaded was the precious mail, delivered so late that it was 2:30 P.M. before *Britannia* sailed.

Twelve days and ten hours later, she entered Halifax Harbor. Although she had carried a Halifax pilot from England, *Britannia* ran briefly aground in his harbor. Only eight hours later, *Britannia* pressed on to Boston. She arrived two days later on July 18, having completed a record crossing—two weeks and eight hours.

Britannia's late-night arrival dampened the city's reception. But three days later, Boston proclaimed "Cunard Festival Day" and 2,300 attended a banquet in Cunard's honor. Captain Woodruff was presented with a giant silver loving cup that, identified ever since as The Boston Cup, remains a cherished company relic.

Nautically, the introduction of steam was unsettling. For centuries, canvas, spars, blocks, masts, and cordage had driven the world's ships. Now that pristine technology was disrupted by coal, machinery, noise, and smoke. Welsh anthracite permeated the vessel with a pall of gritty dust. Boiler-room heat parched the ships' timbers, which required hosing down regularly. Paradoxically, dry rot was more pernicious in steamers than sailing vessels; according to one chief, their wooden hulls started sagging amidships after relatively few years of service.

Alien hands came aboard. These engineers, stokers, wipers, coal passers, and water tenders were atypical crewmen of sallow complexion who normally toiled far from midocean sun. Traditional sailors—shellbacks—resented these intruders and a Liverpool waterfront jibe disparaged "sailors who gave up the sea to go into steam."

Paddle wheels—protected by oceangoing fenders called sponsons—awkwardly increased the vessel's beam. Alongside was no longer really alongside but separated from the pier by cumbersome protrusions. Under way, if prevailing winds blew on the port beam, low-sided starboard paddles took a deeper bite of water, skewing the hull slightly to port. Helmsmen learned to compensate for that continuous deflection.

Entering harbor, the traditional venue of sailing command aft on the quarterdeck aft was useless. However, forward vantage points were obscured by raised sponsons. A catwalk bridge was added to connect the two flanking half-rounds, permitting the master to cross quickly from port to starboard while maneuvering in-port; hence the origin of today's bridge.

One sobering aspect of Cunard's nascent fleet was its vulnerability. Displacing 1,154 tons, *Britannia*-class vessels were more like Irish mail-boats, inadequate for transatlantic work. Winter crossings were so fearsome that Cunard's rivals eschewed them altogether. Sailing westbound in January 1842, *Britannia*'s starboard sponson was so decimated by gales that the naked paddles churned salt spray up onto the vessel's funnel. One lifeboat was reduced to kindling. In the summer of 1843, eastbound *Columbia* was reported two days overdue at Halifax. The worrisome wait ended only after *Acadia*, inbound from Liverpool, resolved the mystery. She had spied *Columbia* pinioned on a Seal Island reef called the Devil's Limb. Although all eighty-three passengers and crew were rescued and every precious mail sack retrieved, *Columbia* was a total loss. Six years later, *Hibernia* came to temporary grief, grounding off Cape Cod so badly that she returned to New York for repairs.

But regardless, the service was exemplary. The line's motto was "Speed, Comfort, and Safety" and it was the third watchword that obsessed the founder. His instructions to Cunard masters were unequivocal: "Your ship is loaded, take her; speed is nothing, follow your own road, deliver her safe, bring her back safe—safety is all that is required." Outbound Cunarders crossed at latitude forty-three degrees north and adhered to forty-two on their return. That strict sixty-mile separation persisted through the final voyages of both *Queens*.

Thanks to Samuel's prudence, Cunard Line gained the invaluable sobriquet "the company that never lost a life." An Atlantic legend had begun.

King of the Atlantic

*As things stand now, it is scarcely possible,
in the absence of any remarkable invention,
that the speed of our Atlantic voyages
can be materially increased.*

—*The Times of London*, August 27, 1852

Samuel Cunard's overriding preoccupation was delivery of the mails; his human cargo was of secondary importance. Though the word "passenger" was conspicuously absent from his contract, rules about mail were fulsomely articulated.

The Royal Navy mail officer was God. Assigned to every Cunarder, he could, if he deemed it necessary, override the master. No ship sailed without his approval. Prompt departures and arrivals were mandatory and severe fines were imposed for delays. A missed sailing cost Cunard £15,000, and a £500-per-day fine was levied for delays over twelve hours.

Small wonder that Samuel Cunard fretted about schedules. Hazards beyond his control included hurricanes, winter gales, summer fogs, and the probability of Boston's harbor icing over. In January 1843, it froze solid, bottling everything up in port. Bostonians cut a seven-mile channel out to the sea buoy so that *Britannia* could sail, accompanied by cheering outriders on skates and sleighs. A lesson learned, Cunard transferred his American operations to New York. New England was dismayed.

Though crossings were made longer, the ice-free Hudson offered incalculable advantages. In the summer of 1847, *Hibernia* tied up at Jersey City, a temporary destination until Samuel Cunard's East River pier was established. His pioneering move would be duplicated by rivals to come.

At the same time he abandoned Boston, the founder moved permanently from Halifax to Bush Hill House north of London. His son William remained in Newfoundland; to this day, S. Cunard Company sells fuel oil from their Lower Water Street depot.

Cunard's shipboard accommodations were scarcely luxurious, with onboard ambiance more Spartan than Lucullan. In truth, cosseting was unnecessary because throughout the 1840s Cunard's was the only game in town. Typically, the company provided no table napkins. "Going to sea," opined David MacIver, "is a hardship. . . . If people want to wipe their mouths at a ship's table,

they can use their pocket handkerchief." However plebean, Cunard's incomparable trade-off was guaranteed arrival.

Ambitious competitors sought to capitalize on Cunard's bare-bones indifference and abrogate the front-runner's monopoly. One such was Edward Knight Collins, an American shipping mogul whose coastal packets were famously elegant. Flush with a fortune from that trade, Collins determined to surpass Cunard.

After obtaining a congressional mail subsidy in 1850, his first transatlantic steamship, *Atlantic,* reached Liverpool in record time. By year's end, three additional Collins Line vessels—*Baltic, Arctic,* and *Pacific*—had entered service. All were larger than Cunarders. *Atlantic* was 300 feet (91.5 meters) overall with a generous beam of 45 feet (13.75 meters)—73 feet (22 meters) including her sponsons. She boasted the North Atlantic's first vertical cutwater. A red racing stripe encircled the hull and her triton figurehead was supported by twin mermaids. Funnel livery was, impertinently, the inverse of Cunard's—black shafts with a vibrant red band at the summit.

Averaging a brisk twelve knots, Collins vessels offered steam heating as well as interior decoration several cuts above Cunard's. Rose and satinwood paneling, extravagant upholstery, and beveled plate-glass mirrors enriched the saloon; the barbershop came with an elevating hydraulic chair. But to be fair, Collins's extravagant décor was deployed mainly for in-port show. Once Sandy Hook or Mersey lightships were cleared, brocade and crystal were supplanted by mundane canvas and tin. But rest assured, napkins adorned every dining table.

Since impatient travelers invariably patronized faster ships, Collins achieved early, gratifying success. But though his engines and luxury may have outclassed Cunard, his seamanship did not. On September 27, 1854, *Arctic* was rammed by the French steamer *Vesta* in fog sixty-five miles off Cape Race. The wooden American hull was fatally skewered by the Frenchman's formidable iron prow.

Above: No wheelhouse adorned *Lucania*'s bridge, mandating wet watches for the helmsmen. *Opposite*: But the smoking room's coal fire guaranteed passengers a cozy retreat during a winter North Atlantic crossing.

Collins's crew reacted ineptly. Though some tried saving their ship, most made for the boats. The sole lifeboat rescued by the barque *Huron* carried fourteen passengers and thirty-four crew, an appalling ratio. The death toll of 322 souls included Collins's wife and two children.

Worse was to come: *Pacific* was posted missing with all hands two years later. With half his fleet sunk, Edward Collins lost public confidence. Even grander, the two-funneled *Adriatic* of 1857 failed and the Collins Line went belly up. Sir Samuel's fleet resumed transatlantic preeminence.

(That American challenge proved curiously prescient. A century later, Cunard White Star's *Queen Mary* would be similarly humbled by a Yankee upstart when legendary *United States* captured the Blue Ribband in 1952.)

When Cunard's contract came up for renewal in 1846, the rival Great Western Steamship Company found momentary favor in Parliament. But their tender was flawed in that directors refused commitment to year-round service; no sailings between November and April were offered. Member of Parliament Spooner said it all: "The Honorable S. Cunard was the first gentleman to cross the Atlantic in wintertime." Cunard's second contract specified a weekly mail service for eight months of the year and fortnightly during winter.

Although it was the Admiralty's considered opinion that an iron hull would sink, metal steamers proved inescapable because wooden ribs and planking could not withstand the relentless underwater thrust of the screws. The first iron Cunarder—*Andes* of 1852—was also propeller-driven.

Four years after her maiden voyage, *Andes* was one of several Cunarders placed under government charter to carry regiments out to the Crimea. Indeed, such was the fleet's wartime attrition that weekly mail service was temporarily relinquished. One bonus of the trooping charter was that Queen Victoria conferred a knighthood on the founder in 1859.

Sir Samuel embraced technological advances cautiously. For example, he and his partner Burns disagreed about adopting the propeller. Cunard felt that paddle wheels achieved faster passage. As a result, *Persia* of 1856, complete with iron hull, still sported paddles. At 390 feet (118 meters), she was twice *Britannia*'s size, displacing 3,300 tons instead of 1,154.

The company's last paddle wheeler was *Scotia*, sailing in tandem with propeller-driven *China*. Comparison of coal consumption and speed between the two bear out Samuel Cunard's contention: *China* burned 82 tons of coal a day for a speed of 12 1/2 knots against *Scotia*'s 164 tons that produced a superior average of 14 knots. *China* also incorporated Cunard's first steerage quarters for immigrants, the thin edge of a shipboard class wedge that would grow to staggering proportions by century's end.

In 1863, a heart attack forced Cunard into London retirement, leaving his sons Edward and William in control. Two years later, within the same week that saw President Lincoln's assassination, Sir Samuel died following a severe attack of bronchitis. Seventy-eight years old, he left not only a substantial fortune of £350,000, but unquestionably the most venerated name in transatlantic history.

Immediately, a grieving board of directors convened at Liverpool headquarters, never more in need of their deceased founder's wisdom. The Cunard Line was entering an era of siege, tumult, and, ultimately, change.

The Atlantic was no longer its exclusive domain; others were intent on usurping the front-runner. British rivals were steaming out of Liverpool, vessels of the Inman, Guion, Leyland, and White Star Lines.

Additional competition materialized from abroad. Two-funneled *Washington* had departed Le Havre for New York in 1854, pioneer vessel of the *Compagnie Générale Transatlantique* or French Line. Further east, the Hamburg American Line entered the steamer *Borussia* of 1856 into service. That same year, the Dutch dispatched the first of ultimately six *Rotterdams* to New York. North German Lloyd's *Bremen* blazed a sea trail westbound from Bremerhaven. *Pennsylvania* sailed eastbound, the first American Line steamer. Some of these foreign upstarts initially ordered ships from British yards but they soon learned to build their own.

Cunard's directors revamped their building and outfitting priorities. The company's bare-bones passage—however safe—was upgraded. In one sense, it was Cunarders' increased displacement that permitted incorporation of additional public rooms and promenades; but in another, improvements were spurred by the competition.

In 1881, *Servia* was illuminated with rudimentary electric light. Refrigerated provision rooms followed three years later aboard a new pair of 8,120-ton Cunard sisters, *Etruria* and *Umbria*. These were long, racy two-stackers, their towering funnels seemingly ready to shrug off the sailing masts deployed fore and aft. The pair was dubbed by Cunard "The Wonder Ships": "No vessels ever gave their owners less uneasiness than these two."

Below decks, the drawing room was separate from the dining saloon. The ladies enjoyed a music room, while a smoking room accommodated gentlemen. Cabins were larger and a surrounding promenade rivaled the best of the White Star Line.

The final decade of the nineteenth century witnessed the most remarkable amplification of Cunard tonnage. Displacing 12,950 tons, giants *Lucania* and *Campania* of 1893 were capable of twenty-one knots and were the first to shatter the North Atlantic's hitherto twenty-knot ceiling.

The new class emerged as pure steamships, their secret weapon concealed beneath overhanging counters: twin propellers. If one were damaged or lost, port could still be achieved with the survivor. Canvas vanished and sailing steamers joined paddle steamers on the scrap heap of North Atlantic redundancy.

With no rigging to restrict the height of deckhouses, *Campania*'s and *Lucania*'s superstructures rose heavenward, establishing the profile of the classic steamer. But one quaint, canvas holdover remained. Bridges aboard both vessels had no wheelhouses, leaving quartermaster and watch officer cruelly exposed to winter weather. In fact, the bridges adhered to an archaic past, enabling those on watch to check overhead deployment of the vessel's nonexistent sails.

However bleak the bridges, civilized comfort reigned below, including drawing rooms, libraries, and smoking rooms of increased dimension and substantial furnishing. Situated deep in the hulls for stability, the dining saloons were illuminated by daylight from vast midship skylights. Connecting the two mastheads, Marconi aerials ensured miraculous midocean reception of news from shore as well as communication with other vessels.

Here at the end of the nineteenth century, it is worth pausing to review shipboard's momentous changes between 1840 and 1900.

Opposite: Firmly established on the North River, Cunard's Pier 51 was a Manhattan fixture by the mid-nineteenth century. *Above*: Although a conventional Cunarder sailing steamer from across the water, *Servia* of 1881 boasted novel electric lighting inside.

Nineteenth Century Cunard Shipboard

*The crew, on the whole, are jolly good fellows,
willing to oblige and be obliged, being always ready
to take a quarter out of you if they can.*

—Advice to an American undergraduate about to embark aboard Campania

By century's end, shipboard would be almost unrecognizable to those who had first trod Cunard gangways six decades earlier. The substitution of propellers for paddles had rejiggered the steamers' general arrangement, shifting engine spaces below and first class quarters forward to midships, away from propeller racket at the stern. Increasing demand for immigrant space mandated vast berthing compartments below.

Return to the beginning. Share an eastbound passage aboard *Britannia*, embarking at her East Boston pier. Pack warm, serviceable clothing within your steamer trunk; nothing too fine or delicate, because you are confined within a noisome ethos of pervasive smells, spills, stains, and damp with primitive washing facilities. Pier-side friends see you off less for celebration than to wish you nervous Godspeed.

Your cabin is minuscule, two narrow bunks one above the other, paralleling an iron-hard horsehair sofa. Although a three-drawer washstand holds some of your wardrobe, most clothing remains in your steamer trunk parked beneath the sofa. Finery destined for London should be segregated within another trunk consigned to the hold.

A covered chamberpot remains a cherished cabin perquisite because *Britannia*'s lavatories are out on deck, an invariably damp nocturnal excursion. Though cabin stewards are plentiful, only one stewardess can be found. The solitary night steward's task, at 10:00 P.M., is to extinguish the candle burning within a glass-paned compartment between abutting cabins.

Reveille is a barnyard chorus: a cow and goat for fresh milk, hens for eggs, lambs for lunch, and—a silent but essential component—cats to discourage the vessel's thriving rat population.

Apart from a negligible ladies drawing room, the saloon is the sole public room, its long tables flanked by reversible benches. In rough weather, the oilcloth surface duplicates a skating pond, across which cups and dishes slide alarmingly. Raised barriers lining the tables' edges are

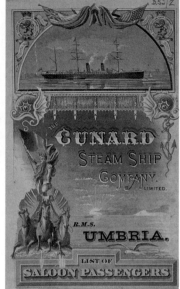

called fiddles; they keep plates on the tables but not soup in a bowl.

Inescapable *Britannia* leitmotif is a tintinnabulum of shattering china; hence, platters, plates, and mugs are the stoutest possible. Stored in a gimbeled rack overhead are decanters, sauces, and cruets. At the saloon entrance is posted the chief steward's advisory: "Passengers unsure of their ability to complete their meal should occupy the end seat on the bench."

Positioned thus for hasty exit, the seasick can reach the rail before divesting themselves of what Cunard characterizes euphemistically as "a tribute to Neptune."

Three days into the crossing, salt fish and meat take center stage. Food is plentiful. Breakfast, at 6:00 A.M., might be steak washed down with a bottle of hock. Heralded by the jangle of a hand bell, lunch appears at 1:00 P.M. with an early dinner to follow at 5:00 P.M.

There is nowhere to roam. Gentlemen enjoy a postprandial cheroot on deck, huddled for warmth around engine room skylights. Below, passenger options include either the cabin's isolation or within that perennial shipboard beehive, the saloon.

Stewards replace mealtimes' oilcloth with green baize for companionable games of whist. Chained to the wall is a piano, cocooned within a padded case, at which amateur players entertain their fellow passengers to distraction. Every Sunday, when the master conducts divine services, the instrument accompanies heartfelt choruses of hymns.

Recreational deck space is nonexistent because the crew must work the sails. Since there is nowhere to sit, foresighted passengers pack folding camp stools; later, they will bring their own deck chairs and steamer rugs. A rare benefit of paddle steamers is that in fair weather, passengers can clamber atop sponsons for a unique exterior perspective of their ship plowing through the waves.

Britannia can be prey to terrifying motion. Thudding into a gale and deluged by torrents of green water, the exhaustion of merely keeping erect, climbing companionways, sitting

Above: An *Umbria* passenger list cover. *Opposite:* Splendid nineteenth century dining perquisite: *Campania* boasted a skylight that admitted daylight down through three decks.

at table or trying to sleep is challenging. Even when calm, it is noisy. Since paddle-wheel shafts must project above sea level, engines are high in the vessel, cheek by jowl with cabins. Plainly heard is the ringing crunch of the stoker's shovel, the gasping counterpoint of feed pumps, hissing steam expelled at pistons' apogee, the rumble of rotating shafts, and the ceaseless "chunking" (Rudyard Kipling's apt descriptive) of paddles churning their way to Liverpool.

Having survived that *Britannia* crossing, embark for another aboard *Campania* six decades later. Now four complete decks are at your disposal, including a covered promenade beneath a row of lifeboats suspended over-head. Things are blessedly quieter. Engine noise, coal dust, and "chunking" are no more.

Cabins are higher above water, larger, lighter, and more lavishly furnished. They smell pleasantly of paint, beeswax, and flowers rather than steam, vomit, and disinfectant. There is a tip-up sink (its water tank replenished by your steward), dressing table, bureau, and wardrobe, all aglow with electric light. A brass bed replaces the bunk.

Yet communal toilets and bathing remain. Since no private bathrooms grace these state-of-the-art Cunarders, every passenger traipses down cabin alleyways to bathe. Bath stewards reserve tub space for half-hour increments. Whereas 1880's Cunard baths involved water warmed, haphazardly, by sometimes scalding steam jets, *Campania* and *Lucania* bathrooms boast proper faucets dispensing sea water. You lather up with a special salt-water soap, rinsing off with a basin of fresh water. Incidentally, whether *haut*

monde or hoi polloi, parading along alleyways in dressing gowns carrying towel and sponge bag is utterly *de rigeur*.

But however acceptable bath-bound dishabille, the bar of sartorial shipboard has been raised for dining. Primitive haberdashery of 1840s vintage—steamer tweeds and flannels—has been replaced by indulgences of satin, velvet, bombazine, and brocade. Once the bugle sounds, dressed-up passengers assemble in a dining saloon that dispenses food exclusively; whist will be played elsewhere. A band of steward-musicians serenades diners.

Electric refrigeration guarantees a lavish selection of meats, none of them salt: Veal, pork, ham, bacon, turkey, goose, duck, calves head, and occasional fowls and game. Additionally, there are curries, stews, and fricassees. Desserts include custards, tarts, pies, puddings, and—summertime boon—ice cream and sorbet.

You still dine at long tables, face to face with fellow passengers. But you are seated now in individual swivel chairs bolted to the deck, chair backs carved with a Cunard lion. Fiddles are still there but less used.

Breakfast is consumed from 8:00 A.M. until 9:30 A.M., luncheon from 12:00 P.M. to 1:00 P.M., and dinner is on the table at 4:00 P.M. "Tea" is dispensed from 7:30 on, with late-night cocoa a Cunard staple. Having lunched or dined, passengers enjoy a choice of brightly illuminated public rooms, a smoking room for gentlemen and a drawing room for ladies and children.

Campania and *Lucania* are without question the world's fastest, 600 feet (182 meters) overall that cross in a record five days, seven hours, and twenty-three minutes. During nine consecutive summer voyages, *Lucania* averages an impressive five hundred miles each day.

However, one westbound crossing of February 1898 proved an exception. Daily mileage dropped to 121 miles as *Lucania* was battered by a freakish mid-Atlantic storm. A *New York Times* correspondent was aboard and he reported to his editor: ". . . Seldom has such weather been known on the North Atlantic. Day after day came gales, fierce squalls of snow, thunder and lightning, hail, fog, and immense seas, one almost unceasing tumult of heaven and ocean. We had sixteen hours of hurricane last Thursday at one hundred miles per hour. The magnificent ship rode it

Above: A rough ocean passage separates a smug steward from his distraught passengers.

out easily and unharmed. From 4:30 A.M. to 8:30 P.M., oil was freely poured on the troubled waters, helping a little but not much."

Captain Alex McKay reduced speed, taking nearly eight days to reach New York. But it is a testament to her builders and crew that *Lucania* withstood the worst the winter North Atlantic could offer, returning to Liverpool triumphantly back on schedule.

The vessel boasts five decks, four indoors and one out, the topmost one called—inexplicably—"the shade deck." A skylight between the two funnels admits light down through shade, promenade, and upper deck to the saloon sited on the main deck. *Etruria* and *Umbria* had a similar saloon skylight but not of this pretension. Daylight illuminates a splendid dining chamber one hundred by sixty feet (thirty by eighteen meters) paneled with Spanish mahogany and beveled mirrors.

Campania and *Lucania* have two shelter decks, the upper deck one less promenade than outdoor corridor. But the one above, a true promenade deck, has been furnished with deck chairs and steamer rugs that passengers rent for four shillings ($1.00) a crossing. Since deck chairs are now of uniform design, inboard legs can be confined within teak slots that keep chair (and occupant!) firmly in place. A card within a brass frame identifies each chair's legitimate tenant.

There are deck stewards in attendance, wind-bronzed company stalwarts who are as hardworking as they are sociable, the brass buttons adorning their impenetrable blue

Above, left: The world's largest liner, *Campania*, tied up at Liverpool. Five-day crossings had arrived. *Above, right*: A turn-of-the-century poster advertises flagships *Lucania* and *Campania* as well as a supportive quartet of older vessels.

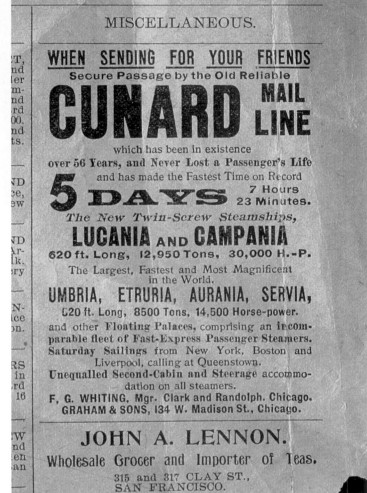

serge tinged green from salt. They stage-manage promenade deck affairs, setting up chairs at dawn, shrouding their occupants with steamer rugs, dispensing morning bouillon, afternoon tea, weather advisories, and seasickness remedies. When darkness falls, they stack chairs into night ranks while decks are hosed.

In sum, *Campania* and *Lucania* offer hundreds of up-to-date cabins to suit every purse. Unrivaled for crossing time, these great Cunarders attract legions of discriminating cabin passengers as well as thousands of immigrants anxious for a new life in the New World.

But however roseate Cunard's twentieth-century dawn, it has been sullied by seismic tremors from across the North Sea.

Teutonic Challenge, Cunard Response

*There was never a time in the history of Atlantic
steaming in which there were a pair of steamers
so far ahead of all rivals as the great Cunarders are now.
It is the Campania and Lucania first and no second in sight...*

—*The North British Daily Mail*, 1894

Mark the word "response." The North Atlantic's most ambitious newbuildings were specifically wrought responses to existing record-breakers. The bleak reality was that every champion's moment in the sun would inevitably be eclipsed by the next dazzling newcomer.

In 1897, North German Lloyd's sleek *Kaiser Wilhelm der Grosse* toppled Cunard's transatlantic hegemony. Sporting four funnels, she combined speed with ravishing opulence, her passengers looked after by deferential, capable stewards.

Averaging 22.35 knots, she crossed in five days, seven hours and eight minutes, co-opting both Blue Riband and the cream of North Atlantic traffic. Suddenly, *Lucania* and *Campania* were also-rans, surpassed by crack vessels of not one but two German rivals; in 1900, Hamburg America Line's *Deutschland* proved even faster than *Kaiser Wilhelm der Grosse*.

A combination of jingoism, hubris, and a desire for revenge mandated John Bull's response. That the Blue Ribband belonged to any fleet but a British one—for which read Cunard—was insupportable. A parliamentary subsidy of £2,600,000 allowed Cunard to construct two superliners, *Lusitania* and *Mauretania*. Each would deliver a service speed of 24.5 knots, specifically exceeding *Deutschland*'s top of 23.5 knots.

New prime movers were contemplated. Once Sir Charles Parsons had demonstrated the efficacy of his phenomenal *Turbinia* in 1897, Cunard determined to employ turbines in both superliners. A preliminary test was devised aboard *Caronia* and *Carmania* of 1905, subsequently nicknamed "The Pretty Sisters." Whereas twin-screwed *Caronia* was powered by reciprocating engines, *Carmania*'s three propellers were shafted to turbines.

After a year's deployment, *Carmania* consumed less coal and averaged one knot faster. For *Lusitania* and *Mauretania*, turbines were the answer. Construction contracts were signed, with *Lusitania* to be built at John Brown's Yard on the Clyde and *Mauretania* at

Swan, Hunter, & Whigham Richardson at Wallsend-on-Tyne.

Take note of a significant newbuilding dimension, the height of a vessel's visible flank from boot-topping to boat deck. *Why?* That elevation betrayed not only deck proliferation but public room pretension as well. The vogue was inaugurated aboard *Carpathia* of 1903, continued with The Pretty Sisters, and achieved glorious architectural fruition aboard *Lusitania* and *Mauretania* of 1907.

Here were public rooms twelve feet high, ceilings ennobled by stained-glass skylights within barrel-vaulted, richly gadrooned plaster surrounds. What a sea change! Company décor had metamorphosed into a serene, country house pastiche, palatial chambers filled with freestanding furniture and a wealth of eclectic period detail.

Inevitably, amplified dimensions and larger passenger loads complicated the naval architect's task. Things had been simpler in two-decker days: superiors aft and inferiors forward, bracketing the galley. By contrast, shoehorning multiclass fiefdoms throughout huge, multi-decked hulls was demanding.

Lusitania interiors were the work of Glaswegian architect James Millar. His first class dining saloon seated five hundred, Cunard's first double-decked public room. Corinthian columns supported a domed ceiling enriched with painted panels. Recapitulating Louis XVI, he upholstered every swivel chair with red brocade.

Whereas the main lounge rejoiced as mahogany-paneled Georgian, the Adam writing room/library was dominated by an enormous breakfront (after Chippendale) of a scale plucked intact from Chatsworth. Only Miller's smoking room forsook his light palette, clad in dark Italian walnut.

This last was similar to Englishman Harold Peto's *Mauretania* treatment. He ordained an oak, Francois Premier dining room, a smoking room paneled with intricately carved mahogany, and a main lounge infused with a Gallic exhilaration of Louis Seize.

Right: A decorative but ominous poster from North German Lloyd introduces a devastating new competitor for Cunard. *Overleaf:* Arriving in New York for the first time, *Lusitania* attracted throngs of excited New Yorkers to Cunard's pier.

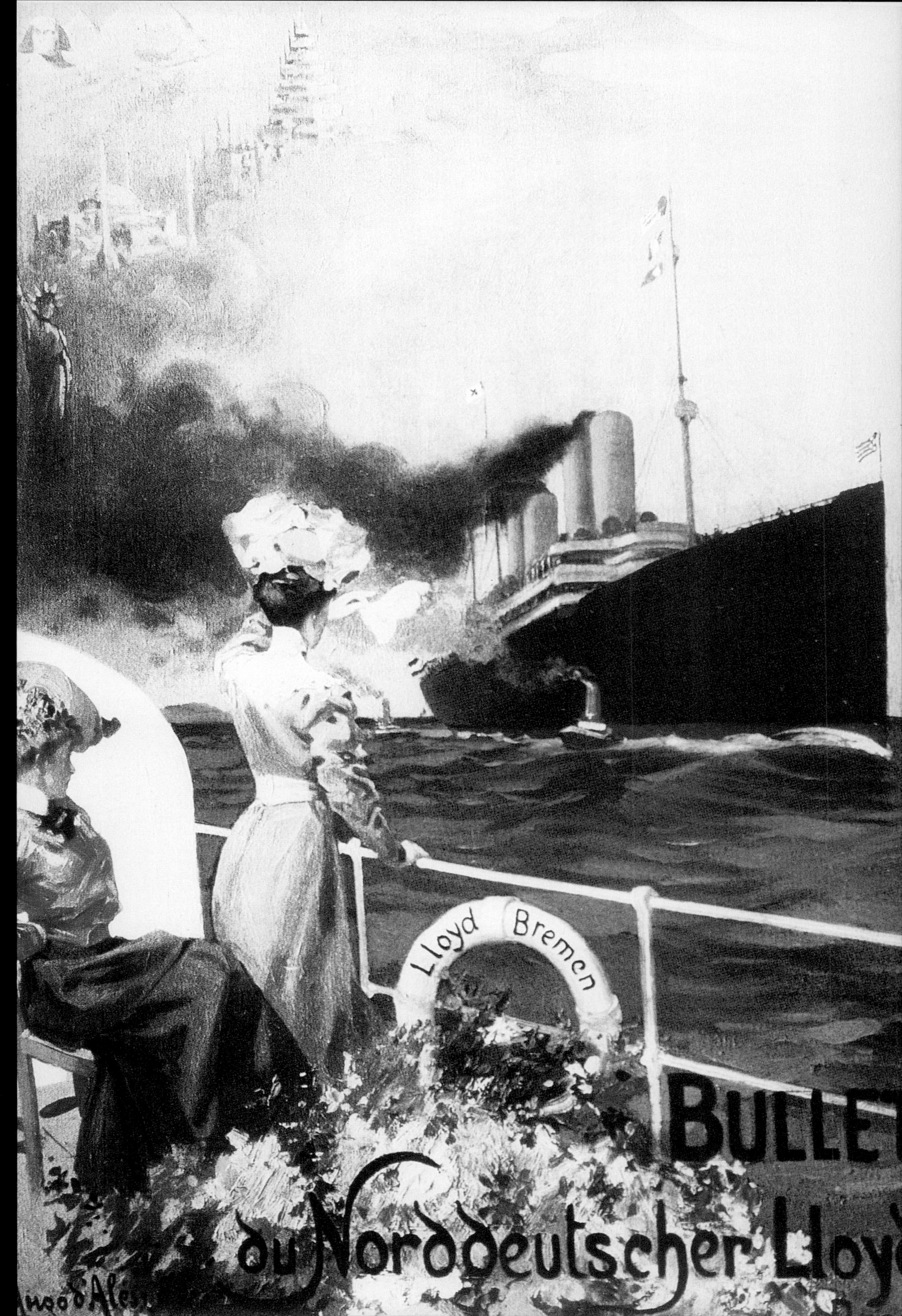
Lloyd Bremen
BULLET
du Norddeutscher Lloy

In *The Song of the Machines,* Rudyard Kipling character-
ized *Mauretania* as a "monstrous nine-decked city." Of
those nine, six were for passengers, in descending order:
boat, promenade, shelter, upper, main, and lower. First class
public rooms were sixty feet (eighteen meters) above the
sea. Small wonder that both superliners boasted twin
elevators, their grills wrought of weight-saving aluminum.

Lusitania was undeniably the prototype—first launched,
first fitted out, and first to achieve New York landfall
in September 1907; *Mauretania's* maiden voyage followed
two months later.

Lusitania was christened by Mary, Lady Inverclyde,
widow of Cunard's late chairman. Logistically, the launch
was unprecedented; *Lusitania's* 16,000-ton empty hull dis-
placed more than *Kaiser Wilhlem der Grosse* fitted out. No
such formidable deadweight had ever been moved before.

Once the champagne shattered, electromagnetic triggers
released the hull. *Lusitania* stirred, her purposely glacial
momentum down to the Clyde never exceeding seven feet
per second. Two full minutes elapsed before her 790 feet
were safely afloat, to the relief of shipyard personnel.

Her rearward surge was arrested by bundled crescents of *Great Eastern's* anchor cable. How fitting that

remnants of Brunel's giant should usher *Lusitania* into
life; she was the first liner exceeding *Great Eastern's* 1861
displacement.

Rather than sister ships, *Lusitania* and *Mauretania* were
consorts, dissimilar products of two competing yards.
To employ favored crew cognomens, *Lucy* was Scottish,
Mary was English. *Lusitania's* profile seemed racier, boasting apparently greater funnel height because her boat
deck's "ashcan" ventilators were so low.

Lusitania would be sunk by a torpedo off Ireland's
southern tip on May 7, 1915, a tragedy that stigmatized
her indelibly. To my mind, she deserves remembrance less
for her demise than for her landmark design.

Rather than scatter classes throughout the hull, strict
geographical segregation was implemented instead: First
class amidships, second aft and third forward. Hence,
access between cabin, public room, and open deck within
each class assumed a novel, vertical contiguity.

First Class was surrounded by two promenade decks.
Only via the uppermost deck could passengers circumnavigate the hull. One deck below, the circuit was obstructed
by *Lusitania's* choicest cabins. Second class passengers
were accommodated in the after 150 feet of hull—stacked

Above, top: Sir Charles Parsons on the flying bridge of his little
Turbinia, the world's first turbine-driven vessel. *Opposite:* Although
Cunard's superliners were rarely together, here are both *Lusitania*
and *Mauretania* berthed in the Liverpool docks.

R.M.S. "LUSITANIA" & R.M.S. "MAURETANIA"

within their own vertical honeycomb—and third class occupied the bow. Their cabins, containing two, four, or six berths, were packed densely forward on the main and lower decks; no third class passenger ascended above shelter deck. *Lusitania*'s pioneering GA encompassed a more complex spread of interlocking class fiefdoms than Cunard had ever dealt with before.

Enlargements were mandated elsewhere. London & Northwestern Railway ordered luxurious new rolling stock between Euston and Liverpool; on Liverpool's landing stage—an ingenious floating dock that, hinged to shore, neutralized the Mersey's thirty-five-foot tidal fall—double-decked gangways were installed; the Sloyne, a Mersey anchorage, was re-dredged and massive new buoys—Cunard North and Cunard South—were deployed.

In New York, though the Corps of Engineers strove to finish brand-new Ambrose Channel, it would resist

completion until August 1909. Incomplete, too, for *Lusitania*'s maiden arrival was Cunard's longer Pier 54. Nevertheless, on September 13, 1907, she steamed triumphantly into New York with—what else?—a Scot on the bridge, Captain James B. Watt. Despite fog delays off Cape Race, *Lusitania* averaged just under twenty-four knots for a westbound maiden of four days, nineteen hours and fifty-two minutes. Two years later, *Mauretania* would average 26.06 knots, a crossing time of four days, ten hours and fifty-one minutes.

The Germans were hopelessly outclassed, the superiority of Parsons turbines proven. *Mauretania* retained the Blue Ribband until 1929, when, ironically, she would relinquish it to HAPAG-Lloyd's *Bremen*.

Neither of Cunard's dazzling consorts was really luxurious. Built for speed rather than comfort, they offered a hard ride. Gymnasium, swimming bath, and extra-tariff

Opposite: Architect Harold Peto's *Mauretania* smoking room. Each evening, atop the octagonal table in the center, numbers for the mileage pool were auctioned off by a passenger chairman.

Above, top: Fitting out at John Brown's Yard on the Clyde, *Aquitania* reveals a boxier silhouette than her predecessors. Her Louis XVI restaurant—no longer dining saloon—was the North Atlantic's handsomest.

restaurant—late-Edwardian refinements about to grace rival tonnage—were not included.

Between 1907 and 1914, four Cunarders delivered the Admiralty's weekly mail, the two superliners in tandem with The Pretty Sisters. But construction of a third compatible superliner was unavoidable. Sailing first in 1914, *Aquitania*, at 45,000 tons, boasted half again her predecessors' displacements.

Unquestionably, this was no *Lusitania* clone. For *Aquitania*, naval architect Leonard Peskett created a larger, boxier hull accommodating 3200 passengers and substantially more cargo. Her ninety-seven-foot (thirty-meter) beam was broader than *Lusitania*'s and her superstructure denser, four funnels surrounded by clustered ventilators.

John Brown's major launchway was doubled and Clyde's waters dredged. The fitting-out pier was extended inland, providing a new bow notch to accommodate this latest, 900-foot (274-meter) Cunarder.

Interiors were devised by Arthur Joseph Davis, a Paris-trained, Beaux-Arts architect. It was a prestigious commission, one that would create a paradigm of serene Edwardian luxe boasting Gallic refinement. Novelties included Cunard's first swimming bath and gymnasium.

First class's Louis Seize restaurant was furnished with proper tables and chairs, infamous swivels relegated to third. It was a lavish space, with walls painted rather than paneled. Blue carpeting replaced standard linoleum tiling. Overhead floated a cloud-filled oval ceiling. Curiously, unlike *Lusitania*'s and *Mauretania*'s double-decked dining rooms, *Aquitania* passengers dined on one dining level only.

But catering compromises were stunningly offset elsewhere. Portions of both promenades were enriched by innovative garden lounges. Brass-studded leather doors kept out drafts, creating unique enclosures suitable for tea, reading, dozing, or midocean chatter. Bouillon or tea was enjoyed at wicker tables and chairs next to ivy-covered, *faux* stone walls interspersed with treillage, fern baskets, and miniature palms sprouting from brass-rimmed, mahogany tubs. With a newcomer's refreshing effrontery, Davis had gentrified *Aquitania*'s promenades.

The Main Lounge was replete with Robert Adam resonances, although unmistakable palladian motifs dominated each end. Aft on the same deck was the Caroleon Smoking Room, beautifully adapted by Davis from a Christopher Wren interior, the only paneled public room on board. Heroic maritime canvasses, cornered with sculpted scallop shells, punctuated the walls. Standing lanterns were festooned with Venetian garnish and topped by dolphins.

It was an impressive nautical space. Wrote one passenger-correspondent to *The Times*: "There is no room afloat to touch it for beauty and dignity." Although portions of *Mauretania*'s main lounge-mahogany were preserved, *Aquitania*'s glorious smoking room went intact to the breakers in 1950.

Perhaps Davis's most compelling *Aquitania* accomplishment remains his treatment of a thoroughfare, the long gallery connecting the main lounge with the smoking room. By placing it off center, Peskett and Davis circumvented funnel casings, transforming humdrum passage into an extended parlor. Broader than many Cunard promenades, the long gallery was furnished with wing chairs, side tables, and occasional card tables. Along its length, potted palms created inviting oases.

Hence were gratified passengers' predilections for the impromptu. Rewarding shipboard thrives on impulse—collapsing into an inviting chair or linking up with friends encountered by chance. Moreover, the long gallery's seated or card-playing occupants were not isolated but exposed to the liner's unceasing passenger *paseo*, duplicating the sidewalk café's vital interaction with passersby.

Rainbowed with flags, *Aquitania* exited Liverpool's new Gladstone Dock in May 1914. Her westbound maiden voyage averaged a respectable 23.1 knots, marginally slower than her predecessors but sufficiently fast for logistic compatibility. Steaming into heavy seas, she plunged just like *Mauretania* but with restrained dignity rather than savage glee.

Aquitania straddled a critical Cunard divide. Whereas *Lusitania* and *Mauretania* were essentially enlargements of greyhounds *Lucania* and *Campania, Aquitania* inaugurated a stupendous new scale, not only tall but also very big. Here was a floating preview of monumental displacements to come.

Opposite: Revealing her graceful counter stern, *Aquitania* rests in Liverpool's Gladstone dry dock.

Three Predecessor *Queens*

I watched the woodwork being made...fashioned by careful, exacting men whose hand cult extends back in many cases thirty or forty years at those same benches.

—E. P. Leigh-Bennet, A City Goes to Sea

Alas, Cunard's three superliners enjoyed only the briefest deployment before the guns of August 1914 aborted peacetime service. Postwar, vanished *Lusitania* was replaced by *Berengaria*, formerly HAPAG's *Imperator* awarded to Cunard as a prize of war.

In 1920, Congress curtailed unrestricted immigration, a sobering cold shower for shipping lines. Huge vessels constructed specifically for immigrant millions were suddenly redundant. But thanks to canny marketing, liners were transformed to attract American tourists in upgraded third class. Because of this reverse migration, postwar transatlantic traffic became overwhelmingly American rather than European.

Cunard was not alone in soliciting this lifesaving business. But as the twenties waned, competition from newer rivals did not. Cunard's primary trio was creaking Edwardian tonnage, grown long in the funnel. For a postwar generation obsessed with jazz, gin, and giddiness, *Mauretania, Aquitania,* and *Berengaria* seemed stuffily anachronistic; moreover, the perennial lack of private bathrooms was damaging. Up-to-date newbuildings were essential.

In January 1926, a meeting was convened at Cunard's Liverpool headquarters to implement a long-cherished company dream, two-ship weekly mail service to North America. Twin express liners, 1,000 feet (305 meters) long, were posited to fulfill the following scenario: One sails from Southampton on Wednesday noon, calling at Cherbourg before racing westbound by dusk. After 112 hours (four and two-thirds days) at sea, she ties up in Manhattan early on Monday.

After a fifty-hour turnaround, she sails at 11:00 A.M. Wednesday, a week after her Southampton departure. Proceeding eastbound for 112 hours, she arrives at Cherbourg Monday morning. A Channel crossing sees her tied up in Southampton by 3:30 P.M. Fully bunkered and victualed forty-four hours later, she is primed for Wednesday departure.

Implicit within that projection was a second ship filling alternate weeks with an identical itinerary. Thus, every

Wednesday, two giant Cunarders would sail, one from Southampton, the other from New York. They would serve as immutable transatlantic pendulums, thundering eastbound and westbound year-round. A service speed of 27.61 knots would fluctuate to a maximum of 28.94 knots, depending on seasonal conditions.

Cunard's unassailable geographical advantage was the comparative proximity of New York and Southampton. Although other giant pairs entered service before *Queen Mary,* a weekly turnaround for *Bremen* and *Europa* was impossible because of the longer distance up-Channel to Bremerhaven. Similarly, neither *Rex* nor *Conte di Savoia* could complete a Genoa–New York return within one unrelenting fortnight. The most potentially competitive pair would have been two Le Havre-based *Normandie*-class vessels, but no running mate ever appeared.

The decision was taken to build the first of these two giant Cunarders, once again at John Brown's yard. Hull number 534's keel was laid with a 1932 launch anticipated. But a global depression intervened and plummeting passenger revenues crippled Cunard's cash flow. All work was halted for over two years until a parliamentary subsidy guaranteed completion. Acceptance of government assistance obliged Cunard to merge with rival White Star.

Her Majesty christened the ship with her name and the largest Cunarder to date sailed on her maiden voyage in June 1936. Although her interiors were not especially daring, they were immensely comfortable and chic. Meals in the glittering first class restaurant on C-Deck—on one level, incidentally—were superb. There was a capacious main lounge, rows of sleek shops, a splendid smoking room, a tiled indoor pool, and, overlooking the stern, Cunard's first extra-tariff restaurant. That Veranda grill proved so popular that an identical fixture was planned aboard *Queen Elizabeth*, scheduled to join the *Mary* in service in 1940.

But another war intervened. Gray-painted *Queen Elizabeth* dashed empty to New York, and shortly thereafter

Above: A second Queen Elizabeth but a third *Queen*: the last ocean liner to be launched from John Brown's historic yard was christened by Her Majesty in 1967. *Left*: Making her maiden entry into the port of New York, brand-new *Queen Mary* steams triumphantly up the North River toward Manhattan's specially lengthened super piers.

both she and her consort were dragooned by His Majesty's government as troopships, an arduous assignment lasting well into 1946.

Only in October of that year was the *Elizabeth*—resplendent in peacetime colors—dispatched on her proper maiden voyage to New York. Once reconverted, *Mary* followed shortly thereafter; Cunard's two-ship service was finally a reality.

Throughout the balance of the forties, all of the fifties, and most of the sixties, the legendary *Queens* remained a North Atlantic institution. Like clockwork, they crossed and recrossed year-round, unquestionably the most patronized and profitable liners ever launched. Everyone who was anyone crossed on the *Mary* and the *Elizabeth*—statesmen, royalty, film stars, literati—as well as millions of ordinary Americans bound for European summers or emigrant quotas relocating to the New World. Passage was inexpensive, fast, and, in the first class, fashionable. Cunard's contemporary slogan said it all: "Getting there is half the fun."

Unlike prior Cunard pairs such as *Campania* and *Lucania* or *Lusitania* and *Mauretania*, the two *Queens* were distinctively different, their keels laid seven years apart.

Mary was more traditional, her trio of funnels supported by guy wires that twanged and moaned in midocean winds. Her vertical stem and forward well deck dated her as well. The *Elizabeth* was more contemporary with two freestanding funnels and a rakish clipper bow topped by a flush fo'c'sle head. All the ship's sinews had been swept out of sight, her superstructure unencumbered with the over-scale ventilators lining the *Mary's* Boat Deck. *Queen Elizabeth's* GA was similar but not identical, her décor adhering to a more sophisticated, late-thirties ambiance.

There was always protracted but fond debate about the relative merits of the two *Queens*. Which was better, *Mary* or *Elizabeth?* Passengers and crew alike remained fiercely partisan. For those whose permanent home and workplace it was, *Mary* was unquestionably the easier ship to work. After all, she had entered peacetime service with a conventional maiden voyage in 1936, profiting from a gentle accretion of systems that followed naturally over time.

Four years later, consort *Elizabeth* had been rushed to sea in wartime haste, crossing a hostile Atlantic with a scratch crew, untested and unfurnished, the start of a twilit, five-year durance before finally entering peacetime

Opposite: In December 1948, the two *Queens, Mary* to the left and *Elizabeth* to the right, bracket Manhattan's Pier 90. A Southampton docker's strike precipitated a rare joint appearance. *Above:* First encounter of the two *Queens* occurred in New York harbor during the dark days of March 1940. Gray-painted, they tied up on either side of Pier 90, just as they would nine years later.

service. Of course, the *Mary* went to war as well but she was readier for it, her shipboard sinews firmly in place.

And however gloriously *Queen Elizabeth* reentered New York in October 1946, something about her chaotic naissance hampered her throughout the balance of her long life. She was neither as easy nor as pleasant a vessel for the crew to work. As a result, *Queen Mary* was inevitably the front-runner, the happier ship, fitting crewmen and -women like a well-worn cardigan.

Their contentment infused passengers as well. Postwar, however dated *Queen Mary*'s interiors, they were always perceived as somehow cozier and more appealing than the *Elizabeth*'s colder patina, reminiscent of a genial, pipe-smoking old friend. The quality of life aboard the first *Queen Mary* is best described as an endearing continuum of unpretentious chintz, gently chattering paneling, gleaming alleyways and public rooms, pervasive seagoing tradition and the devoted loyalty of company servants who made those crossings flawlessly memorable. I sailed on both ships frequently and always preferred, as did many of my fellow passengers, the *Mary*'s compelling charm. And though both *Queens* offered incomparable seagoing perquisites, prototypical *Mary* was always most fondly preferred, a sense-memory that should guarantee incalculable passenger reward aboard the company's new *Mary* as well.

In 1956 came a sinister milestone: More transatlantic passengers flew than sailed. Once crossing time could be measured in hours rather than days, passage by sea was doomed. Suddenly, the honorific "express liner" became tragically oxymoronic.

The glory days over, the company withdrew both *Queens*. The *Mary* departed New York forever in September 1967, bound for California's Long Beach; the city fathers had bought her as a waterfront attraction. She has been moored there ever since, a combined hotel, museum, and convention center, a tenancy that has now surpassed her thirty-one years of service. Indeed, the *Mary*'s remarkable life-after-death is as unique as her original construction time-out on the Clyde.

Queen Elizabeth fared worse. Withdrawn a year later, she endured an ignominious stay in Florida's Port Everglades before being bought by Hong Kong shipping tycoon C.Y. Tung. Rechristening her *Seawise University,* he brought her to Hong Kong where, after a partial refit as a combined cruise and university ship, she was sabotaged by fire. Cunard White Star's former flagship burned through the night before rolling onto her starboard beam-ends, a total loss.

A new and very different successor first sailed in 1969. Suiting reality, *Queen Elizabeth 2* was a hybrid—part liner, part cruise ship, and to some, initially disappointing. Conditioned to the multi-funneled majesty of *Mary* and *Elizabeth,* this ultramodern, understated *Queen* seemed somehow shy of the mark.

The vessel's image, suggested naval architect James Gardner in automotive parlance, was "sleek Bentley rather than foursquare Daimler." Her profile incorporated a single, pencil-slim black pipe above a white plinth. Cunard's traditional funnel color, visible only from bridge or helicopter, had been daubed discreetly inside the aerodynamic scoop, which lofted stack gas away from passenger decks.

Above: VIPs –Very Important Passengers—disembarking from one of the *Queens* in New York include Sir Winston Churchill, Dorothy Lamour, and Cary Grant. *Opposite: Queen Mary*'s rivet-studded flank seen from a New York tug. Her distinctive bridge wing shelters were not duplicated aboard the *Elizabeth*.

Although the funnel plinth was belatedly repainted with the company livery, installation of a more imposing fixture awaited Bremerhaven's 1987 refit, when a massive heart transplant converted the engines from steam turbine to diesel-electric. Accommodating nine diesel uptakes required a more substantial housing, and that engineering necessity markedly improved the vessel's summit aesthetic.

Corporate buzz about the new ship betrayed a determination to distance the exhilarating present from what was perceived as an archaic past. Cunard wanted to shuck its patrician image. "Ships," pronounced their brutally candid marketing mantra, "have been boring long enough."

In the mother country, "swinging London" was in vogue and vanguard designer David Hicks was repainting Regency drawing rooms with his bold palette. Dennis Lennon's *Queen Elizabeth 2* interiors—walls, staircases, bannisters, and upholstery—glowed with the same startling colors. Man-made materials predominated 'tween decks, relentlessly mod and remote from *Queen Mary*'s paneled, vaulted majesty. Coffee shop and disco were in, smoking room and garden lounge out. Restaurants were high in the ship. Stewards wore turtlenecks, their vessel's

name abbreviated to *QE2*, a breezy logo typifying the company's new, informal guise.

No chapter documenting the three *Queens* should end without evaluating Cunard's imperial versus democratic image. Happily, since her maiden voyage, much of the grandeur that *QE2*'s designers had been instructed to eschew has reappeared. The turtlenecks are gone, restaurant managers are back in white tie and tails, royal portraits and a heritage trail enliven the staircases, and Cunard's glorious history is triumphantly on view.

Equating tradition with boredom was a grievous and simplistic error. In fact, Americans—the majority of *QE2*'s clientele—embark in search of the same imperial vibes that also attract them to the Royal Tattoo, Buckingham Palace, Windsor Castle, the changing of the guard—in sum, the time-honored panoply of Britain's royal mystique.

Stephen Payne has wisely observed: "Cunard without a *Queen* is not really Cunard." By extension, a *Queen* without elegance, grandeur, and tradition is equally unthinkable. After all, the rampant lion adorning Cunard's house flag is crowned, conveying a potent regal message. Appropriately, the company's fourth *Queen* acknowledges Cunard's imperial stance.

Above, left: In October 1946, *Queen Elizabeth* departs Southampton on her proper maiden voyage. *Above, right*: A boy and his father pose proudly in front of *Queen Mary* in New York. *Opposite*: Seen from astern in New York, *Queen Elizabeth 2* is topped by her post-1987 Bremerhaven funnel.

Twentieth Century Cunard Shipboard

There is the rumble of trucks and the clump of trunks, the strident chatter
of a crane and the first salt smell of the sea. You hurry through, even though there's time.
The past, the continent, is behind you; the future is that glowing mouth in the side
of the ship; this dim turbulent gangway is too confusedly the present.

—F. Scott Fitzgerald, *The Rough Crossing*

From 1900 until 2000, life aboard Cunard vessels accommodated itself, predictably, to advancing technology, market conditions, and passenger expectations.

That a company renowned for crossing should cruise so effortlessly was scarcely surprising. Traditionally, the Mediterranean had been Cunard's most scenic arena; in 1912, when *Carpathia* diverted to stricken *Titanic*, she was en route to the Holy Land. But it was brand-new *Laconia* and *Samaria* that inaugurated the company's most ambitious voyages in November 1922. Both departed New York to circumnavigate the globe, *Laconia* westbound, *Samaria* eastbound.

Once into the tropics, passengers embraced warm-weather rituals that, familiar to us, were innovative at the time. Outdoor buffet luncheons on deck, canvas pools, awnings everywhere, shaded rather than shrouded deck chairs, exotic ports, dancing under the stars, breeze-catching scuttles projecting from portholes, crews in perpetual whites and—transatlantic workhorse novelty—tenders to shore. A decade later, *Laconia*'s sister ship *Franconia* became the company's world cruise flagship.

The same depression that delayed *Queen Mary* diverted the three Edwardian stalwarts she would replace from under-booked winter crossings to popular cruises. Flocks of new passengers embarked for democratic, one-class jaunts to the West Indies, Bermuda, and the Mediterranean. *Mauretania* adopted a white hull and *Aquitania* sailed to Rio in 1938.

But the company's cruising apotheosis was achieved in 1948 with 34,000-ton, green-painted *Caronia*. The only Cunarder with more splendid than modest cabins, she cornered the upscale market. Significantly, segments of her world cruise were not offered; clients booked the entire, five-month circumnavigation or nothing. This restriction encouraged both *snobbisme* and allegiance, and *Caronia*'s successive world cruise passenger lists remained almost identical.

Between global peregrinations, "The Green Goddess" visited the Mediterranean and the Baltic. And without fail, she disembarked her largely American clientele in Southampton on Wednesday mornings because their *Caronia* ticket included express passage back to New York on a waiting *Queen*.

That ingenious interface of cruising *Caronia* with crossing *Queen* returns us neatly to the company's seminal arena. Sail eastbound with me from Manhattan's Pier 90 for a *Queen Mary* crossing in June 1956. Across a bristly doormat, through glowing alleyways, stewards conduct you to a cabin with lavish closets and drawers, and a spacious bathroom. No more treks down the hall to bathe, although a curious holdover plumbs the tub: It can be filled in seconds with torrents of either fresh or salt water. There is no in-cabin safe; valuables must be consigned to a purser's safe deposit.

Outnumbering the eighteen hundred passengers, thousands of chattering visitors overwhelm the vessel, women hatted and gloved, gentlemen seersuckered against summer's humidity. There is no air conditioning, only oscillating fans and ball-and-socket punka louvers circulating on-deck air. On the vessel's (shaded) port side, open portholes help.

Fighting their way through the crush, stewards deliver champagne, ice, parcels, flowers, fruit baskets, and sheaves of *bon voyage* telegrams. Their colleagues struggle with wardrobe trunks perched atop trolleys, two of which *Queen Mary*'s alleyways can accommodate *en passant*.

A peremptory whistle blast and brass-buttoned bellboys crying "All ashore that's going ashore!" precipitate two decisive adjournments—visitor departure and passenger lunch. On offer are fresh Maine lobsters, reflecting westbound's first-day perquisite of England's Dover sole.

Queen Mary's alleyways are tiled with polychromatic Korkoid linoleum, and the receding squeak of sneakered children racing past is as distinctive as the lounge's chattering walls. Both *Queens* are paneled with the *boiserie* of empire. Every afternoon at four, a string orchestra plays for tea with a musical quiz to follow.

Black ties enrich every evening save first and last; one wears embarkation and disembarkation clothes for those

Above: Treasure Jones, original *Queen Mary*'s last master. After he brought her into Long Beach, he would signal FINISHED WITH ENGINES, forever. *Opposite:* Within a wide variety of Cunard dining rooms between the wars, passengers enjoyed superb cuisine, deft service, and stimulating conversation.

terminal dinners. There is no cruise director, no cabaret, no production show, and almost no audio equipment. Once aboard *Elizabeth*, some talented Maori passengers sing in the lounge, nonplussed to discover that only one microphone exists.

Diversions include bingo, horse racing, movies, or masquerade. There is also much dancing, drinking, and, always, good talk, civilized passenger-camaraderie endemic. The crossing is brief so friendships flower swiftly.

Perhaps the best locales for passenger encounters are the enclosed promenade decks. Morning walkers tramp repeatedly past deck-chaired shipmates, to whom stewards dispense bouillon at 11:00 AM. In fine weather, walkers troop up to the boat deck for bracing midocean air.

Newfound companions or shipmates from previous crossings share noontime drinks in the smoking room, paid for in cash, dollars or pounds; credit cards and cash-free shipboard are decades away. Lunch is served only down in C-Deck's restaurant; *Queen Mary* has no lido, indeed, no alternative catering save for the Veranda Grill or a cabin tray.

Afternoon activities vary. Though the sedentary succumb to deck-chaired siestas, the athletically inclined haunt the gymnasium, hurling medicine balls, riding the electric camel, or fencing with the instructor. The squash court is heavily booked. The inevitable finale is a Turkish bath and massage followed by a restorative plunge into D-Deck's pool.

Opposite: This poster's subliminal message is that *Queen Mary* was not the exclusive domain of film stars and millionaires; humbler passengers were also sought. *Above, left:* Original *Queen Mary*'s Restaurant sported a mural not unlike John McKenna's Grand Lobby bas relief for *QM2*. *Above, right:* First-class passengers tramp around the echoing Promenade Deck, past deck-chaired shipmates.

Long before they turn down beds and draw curtains, stewards have laid out dinner jackets; shoes glow thanks to the ship's "boots." Stewardesses assist distaff passengers with zippers or buttons, summoned by a green cabin button; their male colleagues respond to red.

Paradoxically, there is nothing to do yet not enough time to do everything; five sea days pass in a contented blur. Quizzes, bridge, backgammon, shops, and library beckon. Evenings are dense with engagements as passengers accept cherished invitations to officers' quarters for drinks. In the Smoking Room, Main Lounge, and Garden Lounge, stewards sustain a frantic pace during the cocktail hour. Photographers document the shipboard pageant with black-and-white photographs slipped beneath cabin doors.

France's approach is heralded by crew distraction, re-emerging suitcases, distribution of baggage labels, boat-train tickets, and custom forms. Addresses and itineraries are exchanged, scribbled in passenger list margins. Shipboard chums will reunite throughout the UK or continent that summer, genesis of friendships forged at sea aboard a *Queen*.

On deck, New York humidity is supplanted by northern chill. Three-toed kittiwakes circle the stern where refuse is routinely jettisoned in these ecologically insensitive days. Suddenly, early Monday, *Queen Mary* is alongside at Cherbourg and the passenger body fragments. That afternoon, the London-bound residue troops onto Southampton's boat train, their last glimpse of the *Mary,*

her funnel trio looming above the ocean terminal. That crossing completed, another will begin two days later.

A 1983 North Cape cruise aboard *Queen Elizabeth 2* rounds out last century's overview. Southampton's ocean terminal is still there, its days, alas, numbered. We embark through *QE2*'s midship lobby, encircled by a lime-green, leather sofa. Alleyways to cabins are carpeted now, Korkoid a casualty of 1960s spike heels; all of *Mary*'s and *Elizabeth*'s linoleum has been adumbrated with ineradicable, dime-sized scars.

Cabins are still capacious and paneled, though salt water bathing is no more; the only in-cabin sea water flushes toilets. Promenades are gone too, their width absorbed into a beamier Queens Room. In addition to first class's Columbia and tourist's Tables of the World, two additional grills—Princess and Queens—are extant; no longer extra-tariff, both accommodate occupants of *QE2*'s most expensive cabins. Ironically, the Cunarder originally anticipated as triple-class has emerged with *de facto* three classes—Tourist, First, and Grill Class.

Whatever the restaurant, Cunard's traditional dining expertise continues, an amalgam of deft stewards, flickering spirit lamps, and splendid menus. Every Columbia table boasts a glowing plexiglass column illuminated from below through the cloth. My wife Mary and I share a window table, seated in those well-designed aluminum chairs. Throughout my first *QE2* crossing in 1970, those

same Columbia windows had been opaque with fog. Now, the view is idyllic. *QE2*-size vessels must parallel rather than skirt Norway's incomparable coastline but distant mountains enchant nonetheless.

So do the ports. At oil-rich Stavanger, the ship berths alongside the old town's sunstruck roofs ascending the hills; summer heat propels passengers into both stern pools. Entry into majestic Geiranger fjord is captivating, a breathtaking panorama of limpid fjord and cliffsides laved by the gauzy caress of the Seven Sisters waterfalls.

Across the Arctic Circle, perpetual daylight creates a surreal shipboard mood. Anchored off Honnigsvag, North Cape's port, Mary and I, in evening dress and dinner jacket respectively, loll in deck chairs at midnight, coffee tray in lap, bewitched by daylight's winsome nocturnal intrusion.

Norway's coast was the earliest cruise ships' prime destination, and that midsummer Nordic magic still compels, perfectly attuned to *QE2*'s gentler cruising pace. Leslie, a longtime steward friend in the Queens Grill bar, always knew when we were at top crossing speed because the drinks on his tray were ruffled by what he called "the thirty-knot wobble." But now, along Norway's coast, transatlantic urgency has been supplanted by cruising languor. It is the same blessed duality—purposeful crossing and dawdling cruise—that our fourth *Queen* also embodies to perfection.

With this distant *hors d'oeuvre* consumed, let us hasten to St.-Nazaire for *plat principale*.

Above: Viewed from atop Honolulu's Aloha Tower, second *Caronia*'s on-deck pool (*far left*) buttressed her cruising commitment. *Opposite: QE2* with Empire State Building in foreground.

Hull #G32

Over here, the yard is getting into top gear and we find some of the best men being transferred already. This may cause a few problems for us and others with ships under construction. It is obviously a major project for the yard and France—the talk of St.-Nazaire, in fact.

—David Barter, Senior Hotel Manager, Royal Caribbean International

The late William Francis Gibbs was America's foremost naval architect, a genius who designed countless U.S. Navy warships and merchant vessels. He is perhaps best remembered for his immortal *United States* of 1952.

Gibbs's perennial toast amongst shipping colleagues was: "To the big ship and everything you've always wanted, doubled!" It has never been clear to which "big ship" he first referred, whether *Leviathan, America,* or *United States.* But clearly, his words served as tacit acknowledgement of the preoccupation shared by everyone involved with a conversion or newbuilding. Were he alive and toasting today, I am sure this new Cunarder would qualify indubitably as Gibbs's ultimate big ship. (Because of the remarkable strength of her hull, *Queen Mary 2* is described informally throughout Chantiers de l'Atlantique as "Stephen's pocket battleship.")

Queen Mary 2 began life at St.-Nazaire at the dawn of the twenty-first century. In embryo, she was an almost unrecognizable assemblage of rectangular shapes; only the steady accumulation of additional building blocks would transform her into an overpowering maritime presence, towering above the shipyard sprawl.

While she grew, that biggest big ship remained the undeniable focus of everyone concerned in Miami, London, and St.-Nazaire, whether owner, company executive, naval architect, designer, project manager, inspection team, shipyard owner, foreman, or worker. All were bewitched, transfixed by the big ship that grew into their lives just as compellingly as she grew in the dry dock, a brooding steel presence that dominated every shipyard vista and every waking moment alike.

G32 was the yard number assigned to those thousands of tons of steel that would emerge from the dry dock not quite finished but as *Queen Mary 2* "in steel," as they say, ready for fitting out.

Charged with supervision on Cunard's behalf was Project Manager Gerry Ellis, a man absolutely germane to

anything involving both the design and construction of the vessel.

Not surprisingly, Ellis began life as a sailor, initiating his seagoing career with P&O in 1978, and subsequently serving aboard many vessels as he toiled up the promotional ladder. After joining Cunard in 1990, assignment to a rota of company vessels followed, and he obtained his master's certificate two years later.

In 1996, Chief Officer Ellis forsook ships for shore, appointed marine operations manager in New York. When Cunard moved to Miami, Ellis went with it, charged "with logistics worldwide," as his *curriculum vitae* records with disarming simplicity. Shortly thereafter, he was promoted to manager, then director of newbuilds, responsible, as he puts it, "for all aspects of both new ships—design, delivery, and budget," an extremely full plate. As project manager for *QM2* at the age of forty-one, he utilized not only his extensive shipboard knowledge and skill but also infinite reserves of patience and tact. *Reductio ad absurdam,* Gerry Ellis was quite simply "our man in St.-Nazaire."

Gerry served as shipyard liaison for fellow Cunard officers Captain Ron Warwick and Chief Engineer Simon Gillan. Additionally, he was head of a four-man inspection team, made up of Cunard personnel charged with implementing and checking every detail of the vessel's construction. Also under his aegis was a Carnival inspection team from the company's London office. All these people, most of them temporary residents in and around St.-Nazaire, shared one overriding concern: to ensure that *Queen Mary 2* conformed to expectations and schedule in every respect. The working relationship between Cunard, Carnival, and their shipyard's opposite numbers was less confrontational than collaborative, a tripartite mutual effort to speed an immensely complex job smoothly along.

Steel is newbuilding's material of necessity. Construction begins with flat, steel plates, delivered in all shapes and sizes, acres of them spread outdoors in gently rusting rows.

Opposite: Sections of growing G32 accrue in the bottom of Forme B. The curve of the bilge betrays this as one of the lowest blocs. Note how much equipment has been pre-installed into the open bloc ends.

Grouped according to size and thickness, they are selected and sorted by a lone Frenchman operating an electromagnetic transporter. The noise of his work is familiar throughout every yard, an abrupt clatter as a dozen electrified, chain-supported heads clang down onto selected plates. Electrically glued on demand to its carrier, each plate is lifted up for delivery to a steel-cutting shed where plates are assembled into sections or, in French, *blocs*.

Ninety-eight *blocs* were required to complete G32. An animation that Stephen Payne once shared with me showed a speeded-up miniature representation of the entire construction process. One after another, all ninety-eight *blocs* drift prettily from above like autumn leaves, landing in assigned positions so that *Queen Mary 2* grew magically before your eyes, her profile completed in under a minute. Although an accurate simulacrum, the actuality was far more challenging.

Much of the steel ordered by Chantiers de l'Atlantique was, predictably, out of the ordinary. It cannot be overemphasized: Everything about *Queen Mary 2*—the big ship that is also a "ship-and-a-half"—tends to the exceptional. By way of elaboration, consider four steel samples adorning my study mantelpiece. The thinnest piece, at six millimeters (less than a one-quarter of an inch) makes up a souvenir profile of *Voyager of the Seas*, cut at Kvaener-MASA in October 1997. A second, cut in the shape of Royal Caribbean's crown-and-anchor, is from *Legend of*

Opposite: Complementary curved bow hull panels, port and starboard, under construction. Fashioning precisely the right complex of curves is newbuilding skill at its most demanding. *Above:* Hard-hatted Captain Ron Warwick, Stephen Payne, and Gerry Ellis inspect progress aboard G32.

the Seas, ten millimeters (three-eighths of an inch plus). Next is a souvenir paperweight of *Queen Mary 2* steel, thicker at fifteen millimeters (a fraction under five-eighths of an inch). The fourth dates from 1958, an imposing fragment of *France's* hull, also built at Chantiers de l'Atlantique; it is twenty-five millimeters thick (just shy of one inch), the diameter of an American twenty-five-cent piece.

Whereas the hull plating of conventional cruising hulls is comparatively lightweight, *QM2's* is substantial. In fact, the fifteen-millimeter squares distributed as *Queen Mary 2* souvenirs were not from hull plates at all, but merely joining members somewhere in the engine room. Ellis explained that *Queen Mary 2's* real hull plates vary in size, the thinnest (six millimeters, the same as *Voyager of the Seas*) "high up on Deck 6 amidships," while the thickest, buttressing the bow, is a formidable twenty-eight millimeters (more than one and one-eighth inches) thick. Moreover, this is special high-tensile steel with superior qualities to mild steel. And beneath the plating, the density and dimensions of the bow's underlying ribbing and longitudinal strakes are proportionately greater.

In St.-Nazaire lingo, a section assembly shed is called an *atelier*, which is also the French word for "studio." Certainly, the exacting labor achieved therein was industrial artistry of a high order. Some flat sheets had to be curved to adapt to the hull's shape. They were passed back and forth between the opposing rollers of a hydraulic plate-bending machine, gradually wrought into specifically ordained curves. The plate-bender monitored the steel's changing shape with a wooden template until exactly the right contour had been achieved.

Most sheets remained flat, deck or bulkhead stitched together by machine welding into large panels that were then reinforced with lengths of channel steel for strength. But machine welding was impossible within sections full of tightly cornered recesses. There, individual welders did the job manually, one stitch at a time.

Throughout every *atelier*, dozens of welders crouched nearly motionless within half-completed sections, hunched over their work like graven images, sometimes so still and preoccupied that their presence was betrayed only by the sudden brilliance of their electric arcs. They worked stolidly, those Chantiers de l'Atlantique welders, hooded, gloved, and aproned against the crackling, smoking hazard of their craft, joining plate, frame, bracket, and column one to the other and into three-dimensional reality.

Once completed indoors, each section was jacked up high enough above ground so that one of the yard's transporters could drive beneath. These are motorized flatbeds supported by multiple, heavy-duty tires. The driver is confined within a low-slung cab, no higher than the level of his vehicle's bed, able to maneuver exquisitely since all his wheels can be swiveled at the same time. With the completed section on board, the atelier's sliding doors are opened and the transporter carries it outdoors to be parked against the day of its attachment to the hull.

Mass production of newbuilds with prefabricated hulls and superstructure sections was perfected during World War II and remains a shipyard standard today. A section is nothing more than a mammoth chunk of ship, much like an over-scale Lego piece but made of steel rather than plastic and sometimes weighing in at over 200 tons (182 metric tons).

Whether part of the double bottom, the soaring prow, or an anonymous length of cabins, few sections are completed empty. Imagine building a house employing shipyard methodology, with each room a separate, prefabricated component. The bathroom's tub, toilet, sink, and shower stall are not plumbed in later but are built as integral parts of that bathroom section.

So too aboard G32. When possible, every interior item within a section—bulkhead, deck, pump, tank, pipe, column—was pre-built in place, installation that would prove difficult if not impossible once the section in question had been attached to the hull. As a result, everything built-in had to be scrupulously aligned. Uniting two sections was not merely a question of marrying one exterior margin to another. Every interior sinew had also to jibe precisely with juxtaposed fittings within the open ends of adjoining sections.

G32's first steel was ceremonially cut by President Pamela Conover on a chilly January day of 2002. She confessed that worrying about the ship meeting its promised

delivery date gave her occasional sleepless nights. But then she continued: "It has been pointed out to me that the one surefire way to guarantee that a ship is completed on time is to make sure that the chairman of the shipyard is booked—*together with his wife*—on the maiden voyage." To laughter and cheers, Conover turned to Chairman Patrick Boissier and presented him with two tickets for the maiden voyage.

Initiating the first steel cut, she nearly got dunked. Heavy steel plates are cut these days by a plasma arc cutter, guided along its path by computer. Because of the intense heat and fumes produced, the steel to be cut remains submerged below the surface of a water tank. Conover mounted the cutting platform and pushed the button to begin the process, unaware that she and the platform would immediately be set in motion. That abrupt jump start nearly toppled Cunard's president into the drink.

Half a year later, enough sections composing the lower portions of the hull had been completed, and it was time for keel laying, a second symbolic milestone heralding the start of actual construction. Flanking the dry dock is a large concrete expanse called *l'aire de prémontage*—the assembly area—along which completed sections can await their day of attachment. The first G32 sections assembled there were the lowest in the hull, anonymous cubic rectangles, each one very similar to the next. Only

the curve of a bilge conveyed a verifiable ship shape. (Later sections were instantly recognizable, even to the layman, either the point of the prow, the bulbous bow, or a bridge section.)

For logistical convenience, stern sections were built upside down. Once completed, they joined other sections-in-waiting parked along *l'aire de prémontage*. Just before they were to be attached, they were inverted in midair by a pair of cranes juggling in delicate tandem, not dissimilar to children's hands exchanging and manipulating string cages while playing cat's cradle.

Those juggling cranes are, in fact, the yard's heaviest lifters. Straddling both dry dock and its neighboring assembly area are two gantries, enormous (inverted) U-shaped cranes that can ride the length of the dock, encompassing the entire *l'aire de prémontage* and dry dock within their eight-hundred-ton lifting capability. The extensive horizontal top of that inverted U is called the crossbeam. Completed sections can be lofted upward and carried over the edge of the dock via the crossbeam. Then the gantry's wheels implement aerial delivery anywhere the length of the hull.

One challenge of designing a gantry is placing the man running it so that he can see below. His position is rather akin to that of a helicopter pilot who, seated at the controls, cannot see beneath. The gantry operator's vantage perch is an enclosed cab, suspended dizzily at the bottom of a projecting jib below the crossbeam, two hundred feet (sixty-one meters) above the ground. From there, he is master of all he surveys. But for close-up work, as we shall see, whenever a section had to be attached, the crane operator relied, perforce, on radioed instructions from men stationed at the appropriate receiving point on the hull, who talked the piece down using walkie-talkies.

Laying a keel in the old days was simpler; a small crane would lower a single length of steel atop a row of scrupulously aligned, sloping keel blocks. That was the primary hull element to which all other parts would be attached.

But in these days of prefabrication, an entire mid-ship keel section is positioned atop keel blocks at the bottom of a dry dock. On July 4, 2002—the same date as *Britannia*'s departure from Liverpool 162 years earlier—Pamela Conover spoke before a gathering of press, shipyard, and company personnel. After some preliminary remarks, she brandished a hand-held radio.

"To start this process," the Conover said, "I have here a walkie-talkie and with it, that gentleman up there"—she gestured to the gantry operator far above—"can be asked to lay the section in place. But I'm not going to do that. Instead, I think it appropriate that the first master of *QM2* should today issue his first order, the order to lay the section of keel." Immensely pleased, Ron Warwick stepped forward and spoke into the mouthpiece: "Crane driver,

Opposite: Pamela Conover initiates the first steel cutting at St.-Nazaire. She was nearly dunked in the process. *Above:* Front row seats for a momentous keel-laying: (*from left to right*) Captain Warwick, Pamela Conover, Patrick and Isabelle Boissier, Micky and Madeleine Arison.

this is Captain Warwick speaking. Please commence the building of my ship!"

Moments later, accompanied by the cautious whine of gantry machinery, that first keel section of *Queen Mary 2* —combined *blocs* 502 and 503 and panel 102, weighing in at 650 metric tons—was lowered by painstaking increments noiselessly into place. Concealed beneath the keel were two coins, a commemorative Golden Jubilee crown, and a silver franc piece, appropriate Anglo-French talismans, traditional good-luck pieces for the new ship.

One down, ninety-seven to go. That first section was positioned at the bottom of an enormous dry dock called, prosaically, Forme B. Forme B is the womb of Chantiers de l'Atlantique, a cubic concrete ditch nearly a kilometer long. At its landward end is a ramped entryway permitting vehicles' descents to the puddled, rust-stained concrete floor. At its opposite, seaward end, pumping mechanisms can flood or drain the entire dock on demand.

Traditionally, that dry dock is flooded for only two reasons, either to move a partially built hull further down dock or, once construction is complete, to free it from Forme B forever. For this second alternative, a great bulwark (or caisson) can be shunted aside, permitting departures out into the broad estuary of the Loire.

Halfway along Forme B's length is a giant step down. The upper portion, furthest from the exit, is for nascent hulls. Once sufficient sections of a hull have been conjoined

for buoyancy, the dock is flooded and the embryonic vessel winched down over duplicate keel blocks already set out on the lower level.

Employing that shallower preliminary dock level makes eminently good sense, as following the move the hull's vertical growth is inevitable. Having it positioned on a lower dry dock level has the effect of amplifying the gantry's height; additionally, the growing hull's sides remain more readily accessible from ground level. The final advantage of the two-step dock is that a second hull can take shape in the shallower space vacated by the first.

Today's newbuildings no longer slide down banisters into the sea. That hurtling drama, historically a moment of celebration and christening, has been supplanted by a surreptitious lift off the first set of keel blocks. G32's first movement—"float-off" is the operative word—was an understated affair, occurring without fanfare in the midst of a weekend night, December 1, 2002, nearly five months after the keel had been laid. It was an odd craft, for the hull had not yet achieved its ultimate bullet configuration. Sufficient sections had been joined together to form what was, in effect, a long, low-lying barge. Terminal fore and aft sections, capped to achieve watertight integrity, served as makeshift bow and stern.

Well before that first move, G32-as-barge had already been laden with some critical cargo. Despite the principle outlined above about sections never being added empty,

Opposite: Seen at night, G32 floats surreptitiously for the first time. *Above:* First float-off of a newbuilding at the yard occasions high-spirited pride among the workforce.

those involving the engine room could not be pre-loaded with mechanical components because the weight would have been prohibitive. Heaviest of all were four giant diesel engines; the alternators to which they would be shafted were lowered separately. In another compartment further forward lay six Carrier chillers, newbuilding lingo for air conditioning units. Forward of that, a large square section up near the bow incorporated three bow-thrusters, each with rotating doors at either end of the tunnel to reduce hydrodynamic drag under way. Four stabilizers, two a side and each within its appropriate *bloc,* had already been put into place. They would ensure the vessel's roll-damping capability, a transatlantic advantage of which original *Queen Mary* had been deprived for the first seventeen years of her existence.

So four diesels, four alternators, and six chillers had been lowered one at a time by gantry into their assigned receptacles atop the double bottom while it lay open to the skies. Stephen Payne's choice of diesel size had originally been eight Wärtsila Wasa 64s deployed in two engine rooms. But they were experimental for Carnival, used previously only on cargo vessels, and they are extremely bulky and hard to manhandle.

He opted instead for medium speed Wärtsila Wasa 46s, extremely familiar to him from both Carnival and Holland America Line tonnage. They are slightly larger than the nine diesels presently powering *QE2.* Payne sited all four within one large engine room amidships. The fact that they were employed as generators rather than being shafted directly to propellers meant that their placement within the hull was a matter of convenience rather than critical (and aggravating) alignment.

The balance of electrical power needed to drive *QM2* would be provided by two gas turbines. They could not possibly be put on board during G32's early configuration but would be installed months later, high in the ship, just beneath the funnel.

To minimize vibration, each diesel in turn came to rest atop specialized rubber mountings. Once bolted in place, each was shrouded against St.-Nazaire drizzle in a blue tarpaulin. Only after all four had been installed was the Deck B section above them lowered into place, concealing that engine-room view from overhead forever.

Shipyard moves are always scheduled for weekends so as not to discommode the main work force. Before the yard emptied out on Friday afternoon, they cleared the surrounding dock floor of all ancillary newbuilding paraphernalia. Towards dusk, when the signal was given to flood, white-frothed river water the color of *café au lait* swirled into the dock. After several hours of influx, embryonic G32 was suddenly afloat.

Once lifted sufficiently clear of her keel blocks, she was winched slowly down the dock, over the now-submerged step and carefully maneuvered into position

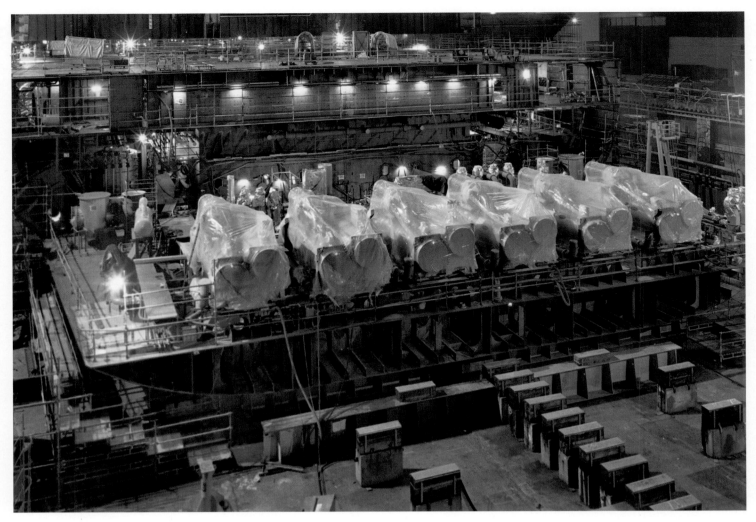

above a duplicate set of keel blocks awaiting her in the deeper end. Some of those new blocks were, of necessity, far more ambitious than the yard's standard timbered balks capped with wedges. G32's after-plating rises high above the keel level amidships to allow an inverted landing space, so to speak, for the pods. Thus, the yard had tailor-made special supports, less keel blocks than keel structures of gradually increasing height; the aftermost one had to be forty-six feet (fourteen meters) tall. All were topped with U-shaped brackets conforming to the shape of the anticipated stern sections, below and around which they would fit snugly.

Once G32 was exactly in position, hawsers to either side were tied off, locking her in place. As the dock drained, the hull settled down on top of the new blocks. Then cherry pickers, utility vehicles, and all the other dry docking paraphernalia were lowered back down onto the dock floor. Forme B would not be inundated again until the vessel's final exit.

Over the weeks that followed, growing G32 became gradually obscured within a scaffolding chrysalis, neither building nor ship. The hull was shrouded in tarpaulins and scaffolding, with welding platforms attached leech-like along her growing flanks. The site was lit inside and out with festoons of shipyard illumination, ropes of high-wattage bulbs burning within white plastic buckets like a giant's string of Christmas lights.

Opposite: One of the four giant diesel engines in place aboard G32 as she was readied for her first move. *Above*: Shrouded in protective tarpaulins, *Queen Mary 2*'s six chillers or air-conditioning compressors exposed in place before the next section roofed them in forever. *Overleaf*: G32's aftermost and lowest hull section hangs suspended overnight from the gantry, ready to be joined to the growing vessel. Note the substantially tall "keel blocks" in place to accommodate it.

Throughout every working day, a perpetual haze of welding smoke wreathed the hull, punctuated periodically by the flicker of electric arcs. Underfoot was the pervasive crunch of grit, every shipyard's inescapable detritus of red-black rutile, a mineral essential for completing welds. Rainwater accumulated in every concave crevice. Pedal point for that construction symphony was the measured clang of a maul somewhere deep within the interior, a dissonant fugue combining the almost human moan of abrasive grinders and the scream of cutting wheels. A periodic harbinger of a large section move was the chattering bell of a gantry leg moving remorselessly along its dockside track, unspooling its black rubber umbilical cable as it approached.

Casual shipyard visitors sometimes despaired of seeing G32 actually grow. On arrival, there she was, the hull they had traveled miles to see, half filling the dock—vast, inert, pulsing with light but apparently changeless. Sometimes days passed with no additions and then, unexpectedly one afternoon, a defining bow or stern section was gloriously in place. Like a jigsaw worried over by a late-night addict, another puzzle piece had been added, and the amended profile was perceived more and more an emergent ship.

Let us document a sample section installation, a portion of Deck 6's cabins amidships.

Lifts are scheduled only on relatively windless days. Yard safety rules mandate that large section gantry operations

cease whenever winds exceed forty miles an hour; thirty-five miles an hour is the cutoff if the wind direction is perpendicular to the gantry's beam. Not only is an anemometer vital equipment in the crane operator's cab but the operations supervisor also remains in constant touch with the local meteorological office. St.-Nazaire is notorious for violent, unpredictable wind squalls christened *bourrasques* by the locals.

Suspended from the gantry, the lifting cradle—a beam that spreads the load between slings—was positioned over the parked section. Riggers clambered atop it, attached cables to lifting lugs—like steel rabbit ears—welded in place atop the section, and then swiftly dismounted. No one ever rides a moving section; it is a firm shipyard no-no.

Then gantry motors ground into life and the section was gently airborne, moving with eerie precision over and then along the length of the hull before stopping directly above its appointed destination. It paused in midair until residual swing had been dissipated. Only then did an agonizingly slow descent begin.

A sizeable reception team waited below. (They are called ship-fitters, quite simply because their job is to fit pieces of ship together.) Among them were four "pilots," senior men positioned strategically around each side of the landing point. All four remained in open-mike radio contact with the crane operator and also the operations supervisor, their boss, who stood atop the hull as though on a conductor's podium.

Long before that section's descent, careful preparations had been completed around the designated area of attachment. All soon-to-be-connected bearing points and surfaces had been scrupulously burnished rust-free and clean. Several circuits of shipyard lights were deployed atop the area, for what was now daylight would turn to night once the section was lowered into position.

But the most essential preparation, long since completed, was placement of what are called guidance yokes, vertical steel posts, each fifteen inches (thirty-eight centimeters) high and eight inches (twenty centimeters) square. These simple uprights, like a circuit of fence posts, were sited at carefully plotted points around the perimeter of the landing ground, first points of sliding contact between descending

Opposite: The final prow section is lowered into place, effectively completing G32's bow profile.

section and waiting hull. In effect, those guidance yokes locked the section into the exact hovering position above the landing point, ensuring that its hundreds of tons of deadweight could move in no other direction save up or down. Ascertaining the correct alignment of yokes with the descending section was the responsibility of the pilot quartet, and they so reported to the operations supervisor.

High above, the gantry controls could be operated in one of two ways, either manually or, as was customary at the conclusion of a big lift, automatically by what is called a digital controller. Reading from a screen in front of him, the crane operator can punch a sequence of buttons that produce minuscule electronic pulses, thus lowering the enormous section almost imperceptibly, with uncanny delicacy and exquisite precision, as little as a fraction of an inch at a time.

Suppose the section doesn't fit properly? Sometimes the steel edges of section walls have been waffled either by welding heat or their bearing weight as they stood on the concrete of *l'aire de prémontage*. But precautionary ship-fitting techniques take minor discrepancies of this kind into account. Safety overrides are always built in, steel insurance that can be cut away once union has been achieved. Additionally, waiting shipwrights boast an arsenal of specialized clips and wedges ready to be deployed if necessary.

With the section only inches away from its resting place, binding last-minute adjustments were made with manually operated pull jacks, extremely powerful hydraulic jacks that, unlike their automotive cousins, contract rather than expand. Workers operating four pull jacks—attached by hooks welded onto both section and hull—can snug newly joined steel masses together following the final descent.

Once the section was down and aligned, welding teams clipped electrodes to the steel, donned masks, and, with blinding flares of heat, married old and new, bulkhead to deck. Had the conjoined sections been hull components, they have been doubly welded, both inside and out. Two days later, once final seams had been welded, the formerly independent Lego piece was no longer a solitary honeycomb of cabins but a fully absorbed, intrinsic element of G32's growing matrix.

After dozens of repetitions of that ingenious but laborious process, the vessel finally achieved her remarkable height. By the middle of March, every bow, stern, and bridge section had been welded in place, and Stephen Payne's almost completed profile had emerged. "Almost" because one element was missing: the final ten-foot (three-meter) topmost courses of the funnel. That could not be added in Forme B because, quite simply, unlike any other vessel ever built there before, G32's topmost elements had risen so tightly beneath the gantry's cross beam that no further vertical clearance remained. The funnel top would have to be added later at the fitting-out pier. Three twenty-four-ton anchors—one under each bow as well as a spare—were on board, attached to lengths of anchor cable stacked by gravity down in each chain locker.

We should not leave QM2's upper decks without documenting some crucial machinery installed nearby. Two gas turbines, each the size of a small limousine, were housed inside acoustically shielded compartments just below and behind the funnel's aerodynamic scoop. Marine gas turbines are almost exactly identical to jet engines powering most of today's commercial planes. The difference between aircraft and ship turbines is how their muscular output is harnessed. Instead of thrusting the vessel through the air as aboard a jet, the marine gas turbine's vigorous exhaust impels a set of adjacent turbine blades shafted to an alternator. In other words, that gas turbine duo atop QM2 does exactly the same thing as the quartet of diesels far below: generates electricity.

Situated high in the vessel, each turbine has unlimited access to the huge amounts of intake air they need to operate. Had Payne situated them down in the engine rooms, space-consuming uptakes would have further impinged on every intervening passenger deck. Gas turbines burn lighter-weight marine gas oil, a more refined fuel. This means that when Queen Mary 2 is bunkered, two separate varieties of oil must be pumped on board, one for the diesels, the other for the turbines. But these days, marine gas oil is readily available in most ports.

With no further gantry tasks remaining, it was time for G32 to abandon the place of her birth. Her undersides were anointed for the journey with two coats of red, anti-foul paint. Masked, goggled, and increasingly spattered, shipyard paint teams deployed on cherry picker platforms twice sprayed the length and breadth of G32's lower plating with a pristine, carmine coat.

Once the paint had dried, it was time for the vessel to leave Forme B forever. The river bottom along her projected route had long since been dredged to accommodate the giant hull's dimensions.

The move was scheduled over a March weekend. Rather than a mere float-off, this was the float-out, a significant newbuilding milestone. G32 could not yet move under her own power. She would be handled instead by a total of eight tugs borrowed from the *Porte Autonome* of Nantes and St.-Nazaire, seven working and one on standby. Controlling both tugs and liner throughout the ninety-minute operation was a female dockmaster from the port authority, stationed ashore.

The tug flotilla assembled offshore before midnight on Thursday, March 20, a nearly windless evening. Forme B had been flooded and G32, barge no longer but a proper ship now, rose again off her blocks. The water continued to flood in, and once interior level matched exterior Loire, Forme B's protective caisson was shunted aside. Four tugs entered the dock, and their crews, after hurling messenger lines up to shipyard workers manning both mooring decks, received and made fast hawsers fore and aft of their giant charge.

Temporary generators had been installed on Queen Mary 2's top deck for the move so that lights gleamed through every one of the vessel's bridge screen openings, creating for watchers the nighttime illusion that a completed and operational ship was setting out to sea.

Only after the tugs had her firmly in hand were mooring cables attaching her to the flanking dock parapets slipped. Then, at 4:00 A.M., G32 was ushered slowly and cautiously out into the Loire.

It was a momentous occasion. Despite the hour, Stephen Payne, yard chairman Patrick Boissier, a host of staff from the yard, and all inspection team members were on hand to witness it. Here was an incredible maritime vision, partially obscured by darkness and only ethereally illuminated, overwhelmingly afloat and on the move.

Opposite: Riding unnaturally high out of the water, *Queen Mary 2*, no longer merely G32 but a real ship, leaves Forme B forever. *Overleaf:* The morning after her momentous Loire outing reveals *Queen Mary 2* moored at her fitting-out pier.

Queen Mary 2 Emerges

Our goal from a marketing point of view is to introduce a whole new generation of travelers to the joys of a transatlantic crossing. You could fly across by air in six hours, but six rewarding days at sea give you the gracious gift of time—the opportunity to do wonderful things that you never have time for at home.

—Deborah Natansohn, Senior Vice President Marketing & Sales

When thousands of blue-clad workmen returned to the yard the following Monday, only vestigial remnants of G32 emerged above water as Forme B drained: an array of vacated keel blocks. The giant hull they had supported for more than a year was elsewhere.

Her brief outing into the Loire—no more than a nocturnal shift to another shipyard venue—had concluded almost immediately with another landfall. Escorting tugs shepherded their giant charge into Forme C, the yard's largest fitting-out basin. Concomitant with that brief down-river passage, the vessel's shipyard moniker was summarily relinquished; no longer G32, she had evolved gloriously into *Queen Mary 2.*

Transfer from Forme B to Forme C permitted a long-anticipated unveiling. For the first time, *Queen Mary 2* could be seen in total. In fact, Forme C's southwest corner is the yard's favorite viewing point. This is where shipyard officials conduct visitors to contemplate their latest newbuilding, like proud new parents corralling grandparents in front of a hospital's nursery window. Save for an expanse of red hull visible above the water's surface, *QM2* was unpainted, her funnel incomplete, and no lifeboats in her davits. But at least she could be seen in her entirety, impossible within the crowded confines of Forme B. It would be late June before the hull's charcoal gray livery was applied.

In the weeks that followed, hundreds came to gaze across the waters of the fitting-out basin. Most had no idea that vital components of that apparently completed vessel were still not in place. In truth, not one pod was suspended beneath the hull; *QM2*'s only propellers at that moment were her bow-thrusters.

None of the four mermaid pods had arrived in St.-Nazaire prior to float-out because of the need to incorporate some late-stage design improvements. Exhaustive bench-testing in Nancy, the French city of their manufacture, revealed the need to enforce stricter controls governing each electric motor's oil surround. In order to expedite the process, two pods were shipped to a Rolls Royce facility in Norway whilst the other pair remained in Nancy. The delay was vexing but inescapable; to have attached mechanically unacceptable motors beneath the hull would have been folly.

After final modification and inspection, all four were delivered to the shipyard. But officials there had implemented the move from Forme B to C regardless because they had a proverbial ace up their sleeve. Forme C is a commodious, watery rectangle that is not merely a basin, it is—providentially—also a dry dock. Built originally in anticipation of a proposed giant class of tanker that never came to fruition, it had not been drained since 1972. I must have visited Chantiers de l'Atlantique a dozen times since 1981 and had never once seen it empty.

Contingent preparations were initiated. Well in advance of float-out, Forme C was drained so that its unfinished floor could be examined. After three decades' worth of mud and debris had been removed, deferred completion began.

New wooden forms were built and networks of reinforcing steel bars wired together. Relays of cement trucks wound their way down the dock's access ramp, pouring tons of quick-drying cement that engulfed the steel re-bar supports. Only after that cement had set was the floor's load-bearing capability ensured.

Then a new set of keel blocks, tailor-made for Forme C, were set in place. They were placed atop supplementary spreaders designed to distribute the ship's massive bulk more evenly over the concrete. Since no gantry spans Forme C, keel block delivery was completed by the same flatbed transporters that had brought the vessel's finished sections out of the *ateliers*. Each arriving pod would be positioned precisely beneath one of the four circular steel blanks that had been welded temporarily over the access ports before float-out.

Those mermaid pods are not only bulky and cumbersome, they are also extremely heavy. Each is composed of

Opposite: Supported on a stout cradle, a pod is hoisted into place from the dry dock floor. Coordinated inside and out by radioed commands, the propeller and its pod are winched carefully up to position beneath the hull.

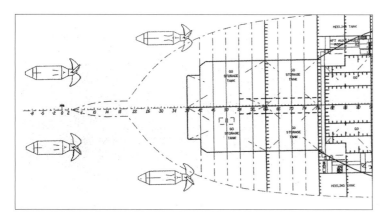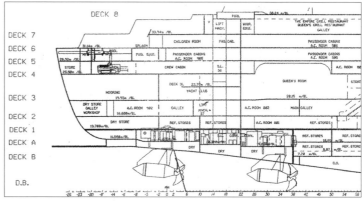

three parts—propeller, pod, and vertical control element— that would be inserted up into the hull. All three combined weigh 350 tons (317 metric tons), about the equivalent of a loaded Boeing 747.

Documenting each element, let us start with the four-bladed props. Incidentally, all seven *QM2* propellers— these four as well as the bow-thruster trio—were made of stainless steel rather than conventional (and less costly) manganese bronze; consequently, their surface will keep pristine for longer without pitting. The propellers' diameter is nearly twenty feet (six meters). Each blade is a separate entity that is bolted onto a central boss. In the event of damage, a defective blade can be replaced, a prudent company provision first instigated for *Lucania*'s and *Campania*'s twin screws installed back in the 1890s.

From the side, all four pods have a slightly dropped nose stance, and the shaft to which the prop is attached protrudes from the pods' forward ends. *QM2* propellers pull rather than push the vessel. The advantage of pulling is that the revolving blades bite into what is described as clean water. Disturbed water passing through a propeller circumference vitiates performance and encourages vibration. For the same reason, the two contrasting sets of *QM2* pods—the forward fixed pair and the after azimuthing ones, designed to rotate to any direction—are positioned outboard and inboard respectively to preserve the integrity of that clean water flow; those forward must not impinge on the after pair.

The body of the pod itself is substantial, shaped like a miniature submarine, and not dissimilar to engine nacelles projecting from the belly of a blimp. Included within the

vertical control column is a ladder for descent into the pod, mandatory for inspection purposes. Being inside a pod under way is, of course, impossible; one can enter only while the vessel is safely moored. Engineers advise me that, at the best of times, maneuvering around a pod's interior requires snakelike agility; despite their generous design dimensions, the motor it encloses is similarly generous.

The control column looks like an aerodynamic dorsal fin connecting pod to vessel. The height of the portion inserted vertically into the hull depends on location. Those for the forward pair—which do not turn—enter the hull on the underside of Deck A and the twelve-foot height of that deck absorbs the entire column. But the azimuthing pair, situated further aft and closer together, requires far more substantial anchoring. Nudging a vessel the size of *Queen Mary 2* sideways generates punishing torque, so their support columns must be twice as high as those for the fixed pair, projecting up through Decks A and Deck 1 combined.

In their joint role as quondam rudder for *Queen Mary 2*, they can be rotated through 360 degrees. The turning diameter of each after pod and its propeller just clears the central skeg, a stout exterior keel extension reinforcing the stern's stability. Motors revolving the pods are electric rather than hydraulic. The master maneuvering from the bridge has at his disposal two methods of reversing the vessel: either conventionally, changing the direction of rotation of all four propellers or, for longer pulls, rotating both after pods through 180 degrees for sustained, full astern power. In actuality, every maneuvering decision is best left to Alstom's dynamic positioning system, which,

Opposite: Suspended from a mobile crane on the dry dock floor, a pod is maneuvered into place. The stainless steel propellers face forward. *Above*: In plan and elevation, shipyard drawings reveal the location and configuration of pod placement. *Overleaf:* Free at last, *Queen Mary 2,* escorted by her precautionary but unused tug escort, sails past the shipyard en route to sea for the first time.

responding to the slightest touch on a joystick, utilizes all seven propellers—three forward and four aft—to move the vessel the most efficient way in any direction.

Placement of the vessel in Forme C had to fulfill two *QM2* requirements: installing the pods while she was perched up on keel blocks yet still within reach of the pier so that men and materiel had continuous access to every deck and interior. Late pods notwithstanding, on-board work had to continue; Pamela Conover's countdown clock was still ticking relentlessly.

Fitting out, the last phase of *Queen Mary 2*'s construction, began the moment she was secured alongside. Her interiors were no more than echoing steel chambers, structurally complete but devoid of decorative cladding. Converting empty shell to finished ship consumed seven months, from May until December 2003, with an August pause as thousands of shipyard workers departed on their annual vacation. Nevertheless, during that apparently idle month, work continued on board at the hands of subcontractors. In late September, about three weeks following resumption of full-scale work, *Queen Mary 2* would depart on preliminary builder's sea-trials. For that occasion, only the vessel's seagoing capabilities were required; fine tuning and fitting out would continue right to the end.

Awaiting *QM2*'s Forme C arrival was a vast accumulation of material piled in readiness on the pier. There were stacks of scaffolding and shiny duct work, tangles of steel

railing, piping of every size, thousands of board feet of teak decking, and crated panes of glass. There were cribs filled to overflowing with a welter of ship chandlery—hawsers, chain, lines, paint, shackles—all the maritime hardware with which bosuns bring a ship to operational life.

Queen Mary 2 was linked to shore not only by hawsers and gangways but also gargantuan bundles of electric cable and compressed air hose. Fed through a lower deck port, those vital shipyard ganglia provided power for workers throughout the vessel.

Every day over the months that followed, nonstop aerial traffic linked ship and shore. Four tall whirly cranes—with less muscle than a gantry but more agile reach—were employed lofting items up from pierside depot to on-board destination. In fact, their swinging jibs had been extended so that they could reach the ship during the time she was further offshore on keel blocks.

One early job for the cranes arrived on a flatbed truck: the final courses for the funnel, which could not be installed using Forme B's gantry. They were hoisted up one at a time and secured to the truncated funnel stump awaiting them.

An intrinsic part of that topping-out was installation of two trumpet-shaped Tyfon whistles, one new, the other on permanent loan from Long Beach's *Queen Mary*. She had been equipped with a total of three Tyfons back in 1936, two mounted in front of the first funnel and a third buried

Above: Workers out in Long Beach manhandle the first *Mary's* number 2 funnel Tyfon whistle and ready it for shipment via *QE2* to France. *Opposite:* The forward stance of *Queen Mary 2* under way is even more impressive than imagined renderings; Stephen Payne's bridge screen is deadly serious.

within the forward curve of the second. It was this latter that had been taken down, crated, and shipped overland to Fort Lauderdale.

There it had been put aboard *Queen Elizabeth 2* for passage to Southampton. On arrival, it was off-loaded and inspected by representatives of the original manufacturer (Kockums of Sweden) before shipment to St.-Nazaire, where it would await installation with its new twin.

Operated by steam on board the first *Mary*, the whistles would be sounded by compressed air on the second, although a token steam cloud would appear for nostalgic effect. Tyfons are of formidable size, 7 feet (2.13 meters) long and 3 feet (1-plus meters) high, each weighing in at a hefty 1,400 pounds (633 kilograms). The heart of the mechanism is a 22-inch (57-centimeter) diaphragm. When activated, it generates a shattering *basso profundo* blast keyed to low bass A, two octaves and two notes below middle C. The unforgettable call of *Mary*'s and *Elizabeth*'s whistles in Southampton and New York were once an evocative postwar tocsin. It is pleasing that the same majestic reverberations will echo over both waterfronts.

Moving about *Queen Mary 2* while she was fitting out demanded stamina no less than a working knowledge of every deck's plan. No interior space was easily recognizable, and obstructions, both physical and visual, abounded. Cable and piping fed through the ship's side spread like malevolent vines everywhere on board, crowding staircases with impenetrable tangles that French workers describe pungently as *le jardin des serpents*—"the snake garden." Those tangled cable festoons, together with a clutter of workboxes, paint cans, table saws, pipes, and lumber ambushed the unwary. Dangling cables and projecting battens underscored the wisdom of ubiquitous signs *Casque Obligatoire*, "Hardhat Necessary."

None of the ship's elevators functioned. Their shafts yawned open, the mechanism of their cars under assault by intent electricians. The only motorized ascent to upper decks was by one of two industrial lift towers servicing the vessel's starboard flank, requiring the constant stream of managers, workers, visitors, and inspection team members to plod up and down staircase towers, improvised hand railings of shipyard piping a necessity. Save near windows,

light levels were low, staircases and public rooms alike inadequately illuminated by ropes of the familiar giant Christmas tree lights.

Orienting oneself to various parts of the vessel was made easier thanks to a useful shipyard trick learned long ago: staircases for crew and passengers can easily be differentiated—the former are always steeper with narrower treads. But the vertical grandeur of every double-height space—Grand Lobby, Britannia Restaurant, Royal Court Theatre, Queens Room, Illuminations—was obscured by layers of scaffolding, erected to facilitate finishing work on every ceiling as well as rigging the hemispherical dome for Illuminations' planetarium.

The promenade deck was a littered, puddled wilderness, the bridge a jumble of cables and gaping consoles, most striking in its extraordinary 50-meter (164-foot) width. (Ron Warwick has joked that he may have to telephone from the port to starboard extremities of his domain.) On cold days, chilled zephyrs wafted the length of open-end corridors. When loudspeakers were not summoning a recalcitrant foreman, they broadcast ear-splitting, nonstop rock.

Welcome relief from the huggermugger on board was a restorative tour of finished cabin mockups in a distant warehouse. There, sample modules invited inspection. Nine cabin categories accommodate *Queen Mary 2* passengers, in ascending order: Inside, Atrium View, Standard Outside with Windows, Premium Outside with Balcony,

Deluxe Balcony, Junior Suite, Penthouse, Royal Suite, and Apartment. The vast majority boast balconies.

Cabin mockups are complete save for clients, their luggage and belongings. Everything else is there—beds, mattresses, coverlets, chairs, pillows, curtains, desks, lamps, and an adjoining, prefabricated bathroom delivered intact from a specialized factory. The moment mockups were first unveiled, teams of Cunard hotel staff torture-tested every cabin fixture. No shred of detail or décor escaped their scrutiny.

They bounced on beds, opened and closed curtains to distraction, tugged at shower curtains, wrenched open and slammed drawers shut. They appraised the comfort of mattresses and pillows, peered into closets, debated placement of hooks and shelves, and evaluated dressing table finishes. They ensured that curtains kept daylight at bay, and that no cabin lights glared when viewing television.

Tillberg's original cabin palettes had tended to a handsome navy blue and dark paneling, but the Cunard hierarchy requested lighter woods and colors. Similarly, trendy mustard-colored walls destined for the ladies rooms were replaced with more flattering peach and rose shades.

Over the summer and early autumn the on-board chaos relented and recognizable vistas of the ship's interior were gradually revealed. For owners and, especially, the vessel's designers, fitting out is cumulatively rewarding. The Tillberg group and designteam were finally able to see long-cherished public-room renderings emerge to full-blown life.

Like a welcome rash, fragments of contoured ceiling broke out atop the anonymous gray steel. This was a time for healing and finishing work, the whine of grinding wheel and crackle of arc weld supplanted by the peaceful scrape of the plasterer's trowel, a time for preliminary skin coats before paint, mosaic, and paneling covered gloomy steel parameters forever. Deck surfaces were transformed as growing increments of bright marble or composition tile proliferated, the product of dozens of kneeling workmen's patient toil. In the galley, thousands of checked tiles were laid, stainless steel drainage grids bisecting the space. Only then could ranges, cauldrons, fryers, sinks, dishwashers, mixers, and yards of stainless steel counters be manhandled and plumbed into their assigned positions.

In truth, the nature of the on-board work was betrayed by the changing accumulation of materials spread along the pier, from the structural to the decorative, from hardware to housewares. Duvets and Frette sheets, specially designed Simmons mattresses, boxed chairs of every description, balcony furniture, rolls of carpet, bales of precut and sewn curtains and bedspreads, hundreds of framed cabin doors, light fixtures, and cartons of towels were hoisted methodically on board.

By fall, interior walls had been sufficiently completed to allow works of art, originating from studios all over the world, to be uncrated and mounted in place. Among the largest was an important (there is no other word to describe it) bas-relief for the Grand Lobby, the creation of Scotsman John McKenna. He is a founder-member of a British collaborative identified as A4A—Art for Architecture. One of his recent works stands before Birmingham's Castle Vale, a medieval tower supporting an heroic knight mounted on a charger, fabricated of sheet bronze and stainless steel. For the Grand Lobby sculpture, his first shipboard commission, McKenna employed the same materials, the sheet bronze bas-relief framed within stainless steel. It is sited along the wall opposite the Grand Lobby's twin panoramic elevators.

At twenty by twenty-three feet (six by seven meters), the commission was so large that McKenna had to relocate to a more capacious studio in Turnberry, south of Glasgow,

Above: John McKenna poses in front of his giant work of art in his Scottish studio. *Opposite*: The Holyrood Suite is the middle of the three duplex apartments on Decks 9 and 10 in the stern. (© Michel Verdure)

in order to complete it. Portrayed is a bow view of *Queen Mary 2*, set against an arrangement of familiar transatlantic icons—sun, clouds, compass rose, and a navigational chart. Salient features of the work are highlighted with buffing and polishing.

A feature of the sculpture is a clock, the image of which McKenna had originally wanted to project onto the bas-relief from across the lobby. But instead, a real clock, its hands wrought by the artist, was incorporated into a corner of the chart, at the sculptor's recommendation, "somewhere near Greenland." As the vessel plies the Atlantic, that clock must be adjusted almost daily.

McKenna's monumental work enjoys a prime venue aboard *QM2*, seen several times each day by countless passengers and crew. One of his logistical challenges was transporting the finished piece from Scotland to St.-Nazaire. His solution was to design it so that it could be subdivided into four component parts, each crated separately for shipping.

No such subdivision was necessary for celebrated Dutch artist Barbara Broekman. The tapestry she had been asked to create for the Britannia Restaurant arrived rolled up. Dominating the restaurant's after end across from the staircases, the finished piece is enormous, twenty by thirty feet (six by nine meters). It depicts a huge, generic Cunard ocean liner from beneath the bow, neither *Queen Mary 1* nor *2* but an evocative in-between, sailing majestically out of New York. Broekman has invigorated her maritime image with an industrial overlay. She confesses that the 120-year-old Brooklyn Bridge—"strong, abstract, and very three-dimensional"—conveys precisely the right robust, mechanistic input she wanted to buttress her ocean liner vision. So a bridge profile, in vibrant red and ivory, spans the tapestry just as it spans the East River, juxtaposing Roebling's tenacious iron web of cable, girder, and roadway with Cunard's bow. Tangles of serpentines and streamers add a celebratory shipboard note.

Broekman's design was made into a tapestry by Ulla Plewka-Schmidt at a Polish mill in Posnan on the Gobelin principal. Had she undertaken the weaving by herself, it would have involved two or three years solo work. As it

was, two teams of four weavers completed the job. The first shift started at 8:00 A.M. until 3:00 P.M., relieved by a second shift that wove until 10:00 P.M. The materials employed were pure wool interwoven with fireproof Trevira, a combination that enriched each color field with a vibrant luster.

Perfectly scaled to the vast space it enriches, Broekman's tapestry serves as stunning focal point from both dining room levels. It recalls the three photographic tapestries aboard *QE2*, originally positioned outside the Columbia Restaurant and immensely popular with souvenir photographers. Over four decades of *QM2*'s life, Broekman's distinctive work of art will serve as backdrop for literally millions of passengers' snapshots.

Four decks higher, the Winter Garden ceiling has been enriched with foliated, painted panels executed by London's Ian Cairnie. He is no newcomer to shipboard work, having completed a variety of paintings aboard Holland America Line vessels. In preparation for *QM2*'s Winter Garden ceiling, he spent a lot of time at London's Kew Gardens where the collection of tropical palms proved an invaluable resource. The leaves of two large banana palms are featured as Cairnie's main decorative elements, and he incorporated additional fishtail palms and orchids into the margins to convey the appropriate hothouse ambience. But since, at ten feet (3 meters), the Winter Garden has a relatively low ceiling, Cairnie did not want to over-foliate the piece. He left sufficient air, so to speak, between the greenery; throughout, he painted without physical parameters because the plaster ceiling his work adorns was made in Toronto and was shipped directly to the yard.

Down in the casino, Cairnie also created a horizontal painting of a 1930s stylized casino. Only eight feet (two and one-half meters) tall, the work is thirty feet (nine meters) long, a panoramic slice-of-life of an art deco gaming club, filled with elegantly dressed ladies and black-tied gentlemen of the period hard at play. Its length meant that Cairnie had to cut his "canvas" (in fact, it is aluminum) into thirds so that it could conveniently be brought on board and reunited.

Cairnie's final *QM2* commission was a series of four pastiches inspired by seventeenth-century Dutch still lifes to enrich the D Staircase. Prosperous Dutch burghers used a verb that characterizes these studies: to *pronk*, meaning to display household possessions with a voluptuous pride of ownership. Rather than furniture, Cairnie's homage to that Netherland *pronking* indulgence depicts prized silver, china, and linen. Ingeniously, the artist has concealed subtle reproductions of *QM2* logos within the paintings, engraved on silver or embroidered into linen. What better rainy-day activity for young passengers than to be dispatched on an artistic treasure hunt, instructed to find, somewhere on board, their vessel's logo concealed in an otherwise scrupulously recreated Dutch still life.

From still lifes to sea lives. Decorating another *QM2* staircase are thirty—count 'em, thirty—canvasses by artist Stephen Card. Although painted on canvas, they are backed with aluminum panels to retain their crispness. Card is a rarity: the world's only maritime painter who also has master's papers. Captain Card grew up in Bermuda but has since relocated to Australia.

A torrent of his paintings decorate C Staircase just forward of the Britannia Restaurant, all the way from Deck 10 down to Deck 1, about four paintings per landing. Subject matters range from little *Britannia* of 1840 to today's *Queen Mary 2*, embracing an intervening roster of company stalwarts such as *Carpathia*, *Caronia*, *Lusitania*, *Aquitania*, and the three other *Queens*. The early-thirties' merger of Cunard and White Star permitted Card legitimate inclusion of *Olympic* and *Georgic* as well.

There is every reason for passengers descending that main staircase to forsake elevators, all the better to savor Stephen Card's vertical gallery. His is a formidable talent; he has twice painted covers for my books. Not only is his touch exquisite, he is also expertly familiar with the structure and history of every vessel he reproduces. Although some of his paintings show them under way, he also poses ships in port, just arrived or about to sail, or at dusk. Beneath lavender skies, the illuminated buildings ashore and the lights of his ships produce a haunting crepuscular vision. That cumulative assemblage of yesteryear's Cunarders is splendidly apropos for *Queen Mary 2's* ocean liner ethos.

Yet another, even more precise representation of the vessel is ensconced in a glass case along the after

wall of the Commodore Club. It is a full hull model of *Queen Mary 2*, built by Dutch model-maker Henk Brandwijk using shipyard plans. His studio is in Valtherhmond in Holland's northeastern corner, and his card reads "Authentic Naval Miniatures." Though he specializes in reproducing originals that float, he also turns out beautiful miniatures of vintage aircraft and locomotives. *Queen Mary 2* was Brandwijk's first ocean liner commission.

Built to a scale of 1:300, the hull is eleven and a half feet (three and a half meters) long, made of oak covered with fiberglass epoxy. Brandwijk prides himself that not one component of his models originates elsewhere. He fabricates everything in-house, from lifeboats to deck lights to porthole rims. His teak decking has been made with an infinitesimal stripe of black mastic between each plank, and every brass railing is capped with shaped lengths of varnished mahogany. All windows and portholes are translucent and 2,400 separate fiber-optic cables ensure that they all glow, bringing this miniature *Queen Mary 2* to glorious, inhabited life. It is, if you will, the modern-day counterpart of the *Mauretania* builder's model, nearly a century old, positioned outside *QE2's* Caronia Restaurant; Brandwijk's model similarly delights *QM2* passengers.

From wall-mounted works of art to human works of art afoot, another first: a seagoing acting company recruited

Above: Model-maker Brandwijk lowers the superstructure onto his stunning Commodore Club *QM2* model. A tangle of optic cables fills the interior. *Opposite*: Two Gordon Bauwens canvasses aboard *Queen Mary 2* show intriguing pairs of Cunarders: *(Top) Mauretania (foreground)* and *Lusitania* frame Liverpool's imposing Royal Liver building. *(Bottom)* Commemorating the April 2004 evening when *QM2 (foreground)* sailed eastbound past New York's Statue of Liberty in tandem with *QE2*.

from London's Royal Academy of Dramatic Art. The idea for embarking such a troupe originated with Deborah Natansohn. To her mind, it made sense that aboard a vessel connecting New York and London—centers of English-speaking theater—some midocean, dramatic synergy could and should be realized. The presence of that young acting company, she felt, would give passengers an opportunity "to see the stars of tomorrow today on *QM2*."

Ellis Jones is executive director for the world-famous academy's New Business Developments, and it was he who recruited and organized the company. As *QM2* was completing her fitting out at St.-Nazaire, Jones and his first RADA company were strutting their stuff in a pilot program aboard *QE2*.

The five actors included two recent graduates for whom that Cunard gig represented their first professional engagement. The resident manager on board is a graduate with an RADA diploma in technical theater arts who serves not only as combined stage and company manager but also provides liaison with the cruise staff.

Their maiden production? *Shakespeare's Lovers*, a compendium of play excerpts interspersed with monologues,

poems, and madrigals that explore various aspects of love throughout the Bard's oeuvre.

Jones has ordained that costumes are "simple but effective" and scenery nonexistent; at stake here is less spectacle than the compelling magic of the spoken word. Other, more recent works to come will include one-act plays of Coward, Ayckbourn, or Stoppard. Additionally, Jones is working closely with recent RADA graduate Tom Foster, artistic director of his own company called Perform-A-Storm; between them, they are developing further Shakespearean extracts designed to appeal to passengers of all ages.

Embarkation of this RADA company was a win/win situation, prize resource for passengers of all ages no less than unique employment for the performers. "See the players well bestowed" was Prince Hamlet's Elsinore mandate; these contemporary players are extremely well bestowed throughout their coveted tenancy aboard *Queen Mary 2*.

Additional works of art afoot bring the Royal Court Theatre—the vessel's primary show-biz arena—to musical life. Cunard's director of entertainment is a transplanted Englishman named Martin Lilly. From his office in the company's Miami headquarters, he has signed sufficient

Opposite: Dancers in Russian costumes swirl and pirouette on the Royal Court's stage in a sequence from the production show *Appasionata. Above:* Though seated high in the balcony of the Royal Court Theatre, passengers nevertheless enjoy a capital view of the action on stage.

singers, dancers, musicians, and technicians to play within *Queen Mary 2*'s multifarious entertainment venues. In addition to a nine-piece orchestra tootling away in the Theatre's pit, three additional musical aggregations are on board: seven pieces swing-and-sway for the Queens Room, a five-member ensemble gyrates in the G32 disco, and a jazz trio thumps away up in the Commodore Club.

Production shows devised for the Royal Court Theatre's stage are a collaboration between two British firms: Stage Electric and Belinda King Presents. Boasting a prestigious track record in casting as well as showmanship, impresario Belinda King scoured the world in search of just the right combination of four singers and twelve dancers who make up the Theatre's multitalented company. Just as elements of *Queen Mary 2*'s physical plant were plucked from a global marketplace, so she sought out, for example, accomplished Russian ballet dancers as well as knowledgeable Argentinean tangoists.

However international her search, the entire theatrical concept is, by intent, purposely homegrown. Adhering firmly to British roots, Cunard's production choices are atypical, stamped with a distinctive Mayfairian elegance

sea miles removed from cruising's customary norm of Las Vegian glitz.

Finally, from works of art afoot to works of art at table. *QM2*'s executive chef is a genial Austrian called Karl Winkler, who served in the same capacity aboard *QE2* before assignment to the new flagship. It is an ironic fact of contemporary shipboard's catering life that landlocked Austria produces the majority of today's seagoing chefs.

Chef Winkler's menus are enriched by some inspired input from celebrated chef Daniel Boulud. His top-ranked restaurant Daniel remains indisputably New York gastronomes' destination of choice. Other Boulud-inspired caravanseries dot Manhattan's littoral—the admirable little Café Boulud on East 76th Street and his DB Bistro Moderne downtown at 44th Street. In June 2003, Daniel Boulud opened a new Café Boulud down in Palm Beach.

Yet another restaurateur, Todd English, has created a restaurant on the after end of Deck 8, the equivalent shipboard venue of the popular Veranda Grill aboard the original *Queen Mary*. English is not only a chef but a prolific entrepreneur, having established a chain of successful

Above: Britannia Restaurant steward Ibo Bekar poses proudly bearing a double handful of entrees. *Right:* The view from the top of the starboard staircase connecting two levels of the Britannia Restaurant.

restaurants throughout the northeastern United States. His first, opened in 1989, was Olives, such an enviable hit that duplicate Olives sprang up not only in New York, Las Vegas, Washington, and Aspen, but internationally as well; Olives Tokyo debuted the year before *Queen Mary 2*. Additional Todd English restaurants include Figs (eclectic pizzas and handmade pastas a specialty) as well as steak-houses, and most recently Kingfish, a Boston sea-food establishment, the forerunner of Seattle's Fish Club.

Since English's mother was Italian, his menu preoccupation aboard *Queen Mary 2* veers predictably toward the Mediterranean. The palette designteam chose for his restaurant pays homage to the lustrous sheen of an eggplant. That rich aubergine tone has been replicated on polished plaster walls as well as in the Travira upholstery covering high-backed banquettes; it extends to the cloths adorning every table. Interspersed along the banquette rows are handsome vertical dividers of sheer, gold fabric columns. Chair backs and seats are covered with a fine gray-and-white check and underfoot is a polychromatic patterned carpet.

One hundred fifty-six passengers are accommodated indoors and—warm-weather bonus—an additional fifty-two can be seated out on Deck 8's terrace overlooking the stern. This is an *al fresco* advantage denied their forebears in the Veranda Grill, an option more likely to hold sway during *QM2*'s cruising rather than crossing mode.

Shipboard's archetypal triad is vessel, crew, and passengers, in that order. One pivotal, last-minute embarkation aboard *Queen Mary 2* at St.-Nazaire was 1,350 members of her crew. Of that complement, 350 were cabin or dining room stewards, the shipboard department with whom passengers experience the most telling symbiosis.

Although a third of those stewards had been transferred from *Caronia* or *QE2,* the balance was recruited anew. Charged with bringing them up to snuff was Irishman John McGirl. He started his Cunard career as a steward aboard *Queen Elizabeth 2* in 1987 and, four years later, moved shore-side to help with training. In preparation for crewing *Queen Mary 2,* three separate steward recruitment and training centers were established, one in Manila, another in Southampton, and the third at St.-Nazaire.

Stewards who had already served aboard Cunarders needed no more than a two-day orientation about their new home. But newcomers underwent a rigorous ten-day indoctrination, inculcated into what McGirl and his colleagues have codified as Cunard's White Star service, imparting every aspect of the company's exacting dining room protocol. Neophyte stewards were drilled about the vessel's menus, preparing table linen, setting and clearing tables to formula, and all the rituals of classic French service.

Heading much of that crew would be Hotel Manager Thomas Rennesland, a man prone to exclaim feelingly, "I have the most exciting new job in the world!" Provision rooms started filling in France, to be restocked again in England. Together with Food and Beverage Manager Guy Sharp, Rennesland made exacting preparations for gala Southampton banquets to come, as well as bringing their entire operation up to speed for January's maiden voyage.

Cunard's corporate executive chef is Karl Muhlberger. His culinary career started ashore; he once founded his own one-star Michelin restaurant—La Tour—just outside Vienna. Then the sea called, first aboard a private yacht, then spells with various cruise lines that ultimately included Seabourn and Cunard.

Last summer, he worked hand-in-glove with *QM2*'s Executive Chef Karl Winkler, devising and refining menus for *Queen Mary 2*. Muhlberger's office at Miami headquarters

Opposite: Hotel Manager Thomas Rennesland poses with senior members of his staff: *(left to right)* Food and Beverage Manager Guy Sharp, Cruise Director Ray Rouse, Executive Chef Karl Winkler, Rennesland, Chief Purser Jonathan Leavor, and Executive Housekeeper Vicky Summers. *Above, left:* Daniel Boulud will oversee all *Queen Mary 2* menus. *Above, right:* Todd English poses with his signature fare, a plate of olives.

boasts no cooking facilities, but aboard *QE2,* he and Winkler reap the advantages of provisions, a galley, and cooking staff.

Both Muhlberger and Winkler were on board *QE2* in the summer of 2003. With corporate distractions at bay, the two colleagues, resplendent in starched whites, pondered existing Cunard dishes and experimented tirelessly with new ones. From cooking to keypad—laptop computers are indispensable facts of life for peripatetic chefs' rehearsal.

Cunard's Director of Enrichment Mary Thomas rehearsed as well, making a September crossing with the RADA company. They were rapturously received, not only for their Shakespearian verse and song in the Queens Room but additionally, a standing-room-only workshop in the Grand Lounge. How fitting that both gastronomic and entertainment refinements destined for *QM2* should infuse galley and lounges of *QE2!*

Major rehearsals of a different sort—sea trials—test all a newbuilding's systems under way. The September builder's trials marked *Queen Mary 2*'s maiden venture under power, departing Forme C on Thursday afternoon, September 25, as a fully functioning vessel.

A French master commanded the four-hundred-man shipyard crew. Also aboard were Cunard's senior officers, the naval architect, and both the yard's and Cunard's project managers. Chief Engineer Simon Gillan was particularly thrilled to see his engines finally put into full-scale operation.

They performed flawlessly. Once Forme C's caisson opened, *Queen Mary 2* was maneuvered solo out into the Loire; none of the waiting tugs were needed. St.-Nazaire was *en fête* for the occasion. Hundreds of small craft escorted the vessel downriver and five photography helicopters swarmed overhead. Shores were black with spectators, and traffic atop the suspension bridge stopped as motorists hung over the railings to see the *Queen.* Both Tyfon whistles vented their first public utterance, echoing across the water.

Over the next three days, forty separate tests were carried out. Anchors were dropped and retrieved, gradually increasing speed was summoned, crash turns were initiated, full astern essayed, and stabilizers deployed to initiate and then correct a roll. Final speed evaluation would await owner's trials in November.

After the vessel returned to the yard on Monday, September 29, Stephen Payne wrote me ecstatically, "Considering that *QM2* is a prototype ship, the first trials were an unqualified success, her performance exceeding all expectations"; here indeed was a pleasing testimonial from a proud naval architect.

More good news followed a fortnight later when Cunard promulgated an electrifying news release: Her Majesty Queen Elizabeth had accepted the company's invitation to christen *Queen Mary 2* at Southampton on January 8, 2004, accompanied by His Royal Highness the Duke of Edinburgh. It was a signal honor; the queen almost never undertakes public engagements in January. But thanks to the sovereign's thoughtful exception, Cunard's newest *Queen* would share the same royal imprimature that had graced her three predecessors.

Above The two essentials for delivering a meal to hungry *Queen Mary 2* passengers: a corps of Kings Court waiters and *(opposite)* a view of the main galley's stainless steel nirvana. *Overleaf: Queen Mary 2* on a calm ocean outside Vigo. Southampton lies ahead.

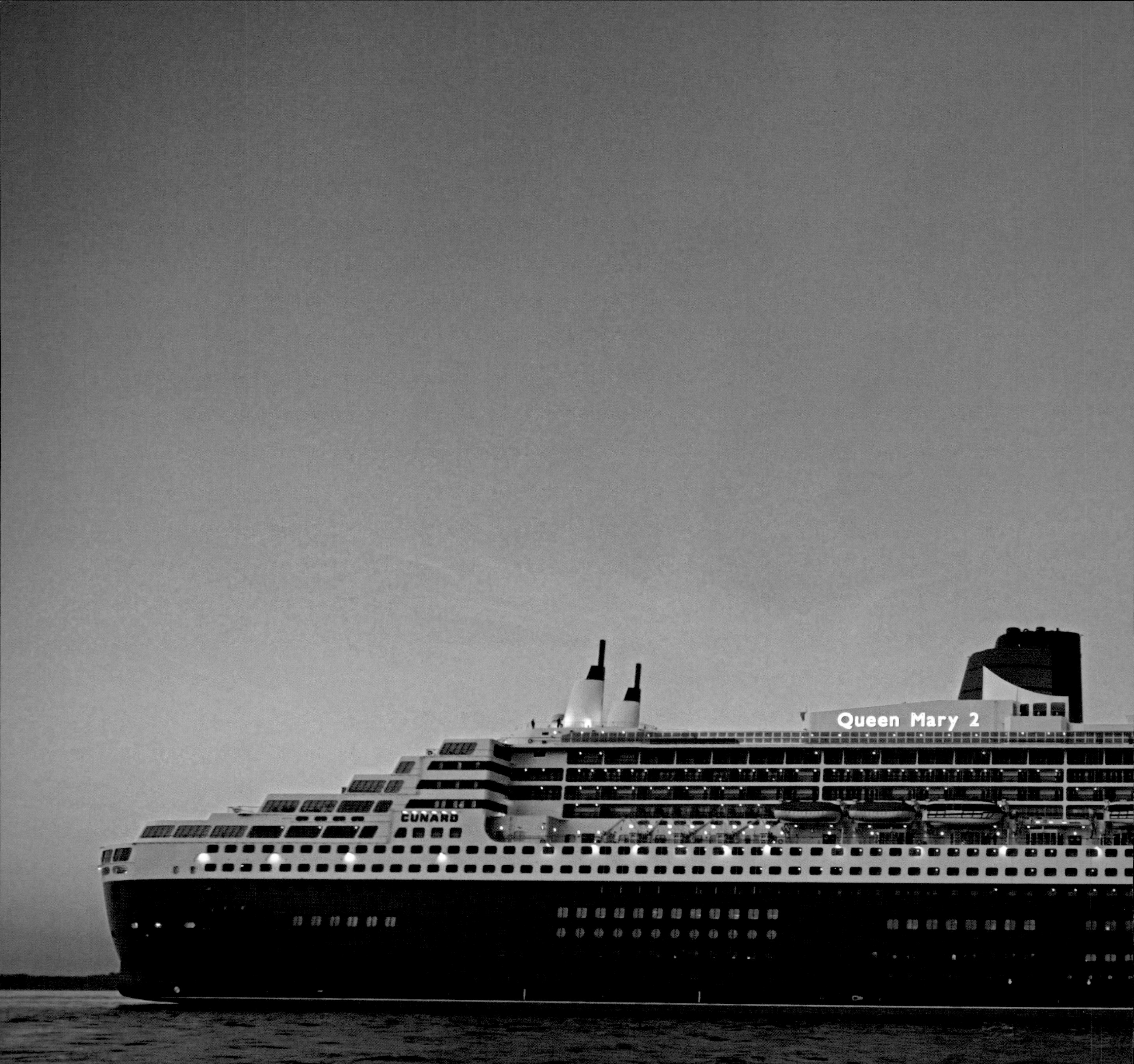
Queen Mary 2
CUNARD

Opposite: Risk and recuperation aboard *QM2:* multicolored chips are stacked in readiness around the roulette wheel as the casino opens. *Above:* In the gymnasium forward on Deck 7, state-of-the-art equipment awaits an influx of passenger exercisers.

Above: In white tie and elegant evening dresses, four dancers caught in mid-number for *Appasionata. Opposite:* QM2's extensive library on Deck 8 has everything—views over the bow, Internet access, books, charts, and postcards, and incidentally, sixteen tons of books.

Finale & Debut

It was the personal service that made the Queens famous, the stewardess, the bedroom steward, the waiter or headwaiter. They were the people that attracted clientele to the Cunard; it wasn't the captain on the bridge, it was the personal service that the passengers used to get.

—Colin Kitching, headwaiter in the original *Mary*'s Verandah Grill

Queen Elizabeth 2 and *Queen Mary 2*, Cunard's two consecutive flagships, were scheduled to meet for the first time in New York Harbor on the morning of April 25, 2004, and sail together that evening for Southampton.

A more apropos venue for that historic encounter does not exist. New York has always been, *primus inter pares,* the port for ocean liners. As the late maritime historian Walter Lord once suggested so aptly, "The ocean liner is to New York what the riverboat was to New Orleans." Moreover, New York remains an historic company destination. Ever since Samuel Cunard transferred his American terminus from Boston to New York in 1847, Manhattan and the Cunarders moored along its waterfront have generated a consistent, socio-maritime synergy.

Now, after thirty-five years of regular landfalls, *Queen Elizabeth 2*'s New York calls will be few and far between, and a recurring Manhattan icon will be no more. The prospect of the vessel's semi-disappearance is unsettling for everyone—ship-lovers, inhabitants of the port, long-shoremen, tug-masters, ship chandlers and, inevitably, her crew, for whom the de facto capital of the United States has long been a favorite call.

Aboard *QE2* that last full summer of transatlantic service, sad finale was offset by exciting debut. A ship-wide buzz—*Queen Mary 2*—dominated every conversation in public room, office, and alleyway. Predictably, some crewmembers were not interested in transferring to the new flagship. Two cabin stewards, longtime Cunard hands, were typical of the disinclined. "Better the devil you know . . ." opined one old lag meaningfully while another confided, "You know, somebody has to stay and look after the old girl."

In truth, their reluctance was understandable. After more than three decades in service, the regime aboard *QE2* had become as familiar as it was timeworn. Working the ship was like wearing comfortable old shoes, and the prospect of relinquishing them to break in a potentially balky, perhaps

blister-making, new pair did not suit the unadventurous. The start-up, as the company's baptism of every newbuilding is called, can be a demanding, logistical ordeal.

But others found the lure of a new ship irresistible and embraced the challenge of embarking on the next phase of their sea-going careers. For hotel manager Jacqui Hodgson, *QM2* is only her second ship, having joined *QE2* as an assistant purser in July 1978 and remaining happily on board ever since. She was one of the thirteen female staff participating in the vessel's Falkland venture; proud adornment of her evening rig lapel is the silver/blue South Atlantic medal. Hodgson is one of two hotel managers who sailed on *Queen Mary 2* in January, together with her colleague Thomas Rennesland. For the maiden voyage of a huge new ship, Jacqui suggested, doubling hotel managers made eminent good sense.

Whereas Robert Cheadle, Queens Grill relief restaurant manager, was to assume the top job in the same space aboard *QM2*, his colleague David Chambers stayed put. A restaurant owner in Wales until 1985, Cheadle came aboard *QE2* as a keen headwaiter and two years later, was promoted to manager.

Maitre d'hotel for *Queen Mary 2*'s Princess Grill is Dutchman Arjan Scheepers. Aboard *QE2* last summer, he was placed in charge of the Caronia Restaurant for some "big ship" experience; prior Cunard assignments had been exclusively aboard the smaller vessels of Seabourn.

Throughout *Queen Mary 2*'s galley, *QE2* veterans abound. Executive chef Karl Winkler and corporate chef Karl Muhlberger report that 25 percent of the *QM2*'s galley staff transferred from *QE2*, in company with a smaller percentage from *Caronia*. The balance was new, recruited from around the world.

Despite the current explosion of newbuildings, the cruise industry remains a very small world. One key player aboard *Queen Mary 2* is Cruise Director Ray Rouse. What sets Britisher Rouse apart is his previous service for ten years as a London policeman. In his spare time, he became an

Above: Heralding the staircase approach to Illuminations, an heroic, life-size Jupiter by Englishman Matthew Wurr. *Opposite:* Lying peacefully in late afternoon sun, *QM2*'s charcoal gray hull glows with the setting sun.

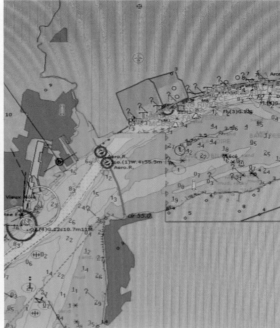

became an increasingly talented amateur dancer. He and his partner (later wife) Lise won several ballroom dance competitions and, as champions, were offered professional employment at sea—dance team aboard *QE2* in 1974 followed by three *Rotterdam* world cruises. In 1977, he signed on as a cruise staff member and sailed as director with Royal Caribbean until 1999, then aboard *Costa Atlantica*.

By the year 2000, Rouse had completed seven new ship start-ups and opted—temporarily—for a spell ashore. Then the Beverly Scott Agency telephoned out of the blue to offer him the plum *Queen Mary 2* assignment, the eighth and doubtless most challenging start-up of his career.

During the months that followed, Rouse was immersed in preparations, responsible for a cruise staff numbering 15 and in nominal charge of 126 singers, dancers, musicians, and technical personnel. Between bouts of organizational work in Miami, he flew not only to St.-Nazaire but also to the British port of Bristol where, inside a cavernous warehouse, Stage Electrics had replicated *Queen Mary 2*'s Royal Court stage.

Starting on October 1, 2003, the production show's cast rehearsed all three revues planned for the inaugural season. Sixteen disparate dancers and singers became *Queen Mary 2*'s "boys and girls" of the production shows, forging dual bonds as fellow cast members and also fellow shipmates to come. Those intensive Bristol rehearsals paid enormous dividends once the company embarked at St.-Nazaire in late December, ready for technical rehearsals on a stage they already knew intimately

The vessel's second set of sea trials, identified as the owner's trials, took place over a long weekend, from November 7 through November 11, 2003. A planned shift of venue northward to Cunard's historic test waters off the Scottish island of Arran was not permitted; maritime authorities stipulated that French newbuildings must remain within forty miles of the Brittany coast. The

weather for those second trials was calm, so calm that those on board were deprived yet again of a chance to see how *Queen Mary 2* responded to rough seas.

Undoubtedly, the most scrupulously plotted event from those trials was the final speed runs, this time—as opposed to September's trials—with the advantage of a clean hull and polished propeller blades. Instead of tracking a measured mile painted along Scottish cliffs, *Queen Mary 2*'s speed was adduced over three consecutive runs with the help of Differential Global Positioning fixes. After compensatory adjustments had been made for wind, tide, and sea variables, the results were gratifying: *QM2* averaged 29.62 knots, comfortably in excess of the contractual 29.35. There were times when she actually topped 30 knots. For the final run, the French master extended Ron Warwick the courtesy of taking the controls. "The ship steered remarkably well," he recalled. "I never had to use more than one degree of helm to maintain the course."

Another interesting test was an eight-hour endurance run to see how the vessel and her system behaved at sustained speed. During the daylight portion of this exercise, Stephen Payne and his Carnival boss, John Hopkins, abandoned the bridge for the stern; behind them spread a unique, broad wake, turbulent ocean signature of the four-screwed vessel. Additionally, Lloyds Register mandated another eight-hour endurance test in a condition known as UMS—Unmanned Machinery Spaces. *QM2* was to function while being operated only remotely from the control room, with no on-site human override. Those results, too, were completely successful. Although that UMS test posited a scenario that would never occur in passenger service, it offered a splendid testimonial to the reliability of the vessel's monitoring systems.

Stephen Payne concluded his owner's trials dispatch on an upbeat note, "Once again, *Queen Mary 2* demonstrated just how capable she is. There was a tremendous spirit of

Opposite: Not with her rudder but with her two azimuthal Mermaid pods hard over, *Queen Mary 2* executes a sharp turn to port, one of many maneuvers required during sea trials. *Above left:* The scene on *Queen Mary 2*'s bridge at the start of passage to Southampton. *Above right:* Computerized rather than paper charts simplify modern-day navigation.

achievement as we returned to St.-Nazaire with the quayside thronged. The final push to complete the ship for delivery could now begin."

As soon as *QM2* was secured once again in Forme C, the dock was drained to permit examination of an errant bow-thruster. At the same time, hundreds of shipyard workers swarmed on board to continue her fitting out. Throughout the vessel over those last seven weeks, finishing touches were the order of the day. Final teak decking was laid on decks overlooking the stern, loudspeaker and light levels were set, paintings and sculpture were hung in place, and every public room, staircase, and cabin corridor were carpeted. To protect that pristine but vulnerable surface from shipyard grime, everyone boarding the vessel from then on had to don blue protective booties—shower caps for shoes—the moment they crossed the gangway.

Alas, tragedy marred the vessel's final weeks in port. On Saturday afternoon of November 15, an excited gathering of invited shipyard family members assembled on the pier for a tour of the vessel. As they were boarding, a special gangway rigged for the occasion to deliver the crowds directly onto Deck 2 collapsed, causing forty people to fall between the pier and hull onto the dry dock floor. Emergency vehicles and rescue workers immediately converged in a desperate rescue effort. The final toll was appalling; sixteen lives were lost and hospitals within the region were filled with the seriously injured.

All of St.-Nazaire, indeed, all of France, was plunged into grief. President Jacques Chirac, who had been invited to tour the ship that same afternoon, came the next day as a solemn gesture of respect for the workers and their families. The following Monday, all work on *Queen Mary 2* was suspended for the day, mute remembrance in honor of the lives lost.

Handing a completed vessel over from builder to owner, described in shipping circles as delivery, remains a deceptively brief but monumentally significant ceremony. On the morning of Monday, December 22, 2003, two maritime/corporate contingents assembled beneath a pale winter sun atop the vessel, personnel representing both owner and shipyard. Chairman Arison, President Conover, Stephen Payne, and Captain Warwick, along with senior officers and corporate staff, gathered to port while Alstom Chantiers de l'Atlantique Chairman Patrick Boissier and his corporate entourage and project managers congregated to starboard.

After some brief preliminary remarks, Boissier ordered the French tricolor lowered from the yardarm where it had fluttered since the first trials. It descended to the recorded strains of *La Marseillaise*.

Once the flag was down, Ron Warwick stepped forward. His sole command was "Hoist the red ensign!" The famous "red duster"—Britain's merchant navy flag—was raised to the mainmast gaff, followed by Cunard's house flag and the Blue Peter, to the accompaniment of "God Save the Queen."

That concluded the ceremony; transfer of ownership a *fait accompli*. *Queen Mary 2* was no longer a French shipyard

Above top: During the delivery or handing-over ceremony, the French tricolor is lowered. *Above:* Staff Captain Chris Wells welcomes aboard St.-Nazaire harbor pilots. *Opposite:* Leaving St.-Nazaire for the last time, *Queen Mary 2* is escorted once again by a tug flotilla.

product but a bona fide Cunarder, on the cusp of departure. Eight hundred million dollars worth of ocean liner, a gleaming amalgam of ingenuity, dedication, and toil, had been completed and delivered on schedule.

There followed a flurry of photographs, handshakes, and congratulations before both amiable entourages forsook the winter weather and repaired below for a celebratory luncheon in the Britannia Restaurant. For hotel manager Thomas Rennesland and food and beverage manager Guy Sharp, this was the opening salvo of a veritable barrage of demanding receptions and meals that would put the vessel's galley and catering staff to the test during Southampton days to come.

Early on delivery morning, crewmembers, scattered ashore in and around St.-Nazaire, relinquished their temporary French digs to board their new floating home. Officers and inspection team members gave up apartments, bid farewell to landlords, and turned in rented cars; on board, they doffed hardhats in favor of uniform caps for the first time in months.

QM2's departure took place the following day. Thousands of St.-Nazairians turned out to witness this final sailing, every pier, mole, and promontory black with spectators. The French townspeople have always exhibited a proprietary air about vessels that come to life in what they perceive as "their yard." Now that distinctive profile, familiar for more than a year above their rooftops, was departing St.-Nazaire forever. Twice she had sailed temporarily to sea over two autumn weekends, but this was the yard's finale, as the largest passenger vessel ever built departed for an exciting debut in Southampton before setting out onto the oceans of the world.

In fact, a generous four days had been allotted for *Queen Mary 2* to reach Southampton, three of them described tersely in the operational schedule as "Operation Shakedown and Ship Prep." Captain Warwick was anxious to try out his new command not only in Bay of Biscay waters but also, as he put it, for "some maneuvering practice in the harbor area." The harbor in question was Vigo on Spain's northern coast. *QM2* proceeded south to the Spanish port and Warwick undertook a series of invaluable maneuvering sessions offshore.

Opposite: A royal collage decorating the Queens Room after port wall shows King George V and Queen Mary as Prince and Princess of Wales at Marlborough House. *Above:* Pamela Conover and Commodore Warwick greet Her Majesty, Queen Elizabeth II, as she arrives for the christening.

Then, early on Christmas morning, he turned his vessel's bows north, racing past St.-Nazaire again, bound for the United Kingdom. An important addition to the ship's company was a team of photographers shooting brochure pictures of completely decorated and furnished public rooms, no longer virtual renderings but glowing actuality.

Thus Cunard's focus shifted from the French town at the mouth of the Loire to the great British port at the mouths of the rivers Itchen and Test. Southampton is *Queen Mary 2's* port of registry and, after her triumphal entry into the port on Boxing Day, December 26, she was immediately deluged with visitors, introduced to thousands of European travel press and agents via a series of tours, receptions, and overnight excursions into the Channel.

In addition to delighting those invited on board, the vessel's mere presence proved memorable to many others. What transfixed everyone who saw *Queen Mary 2* was how high her vast flank towered above the terminal in a way that *Queen Elizabeth 2* never had. Even though yachtsmen were supposedly winter-bound, a nonstop parade of small boats inspected the new arrival throughout every day. Passengers commuting by Red Funnel ferry between the mainland and the Isle of Wight had a capital view as they sailed past this newest Cunarder moored in their port.

Unquestionably, climax of that Southampton stay was the christening ceremony that took place at 4:00 P.M. January 8, 2004. Part concert, part spectacle, and, thanks to its royal patronage, part worldwide event, it was a scrupulously orchestrated occasion that had required months of preparation.

First charged with marshaling elements of the ceremony was the company's UK Corporate Communications Manager, Eric Flounders. When I first asked Flounders the nature of the ceremony that would baptize *Queen Mary 2*, he responded lightheartedly, "There won't be a dry eye in the house." His assistant, Michael Gallagher, later referred me to the christening team, twenty-two strong under the leadership of Emily Mathieson, who has been involved with the creation of christening ceremonies for a dozen years.

Her first task was arriving at a finished guest list; only that would dictate the dimensions of a sheltered enclosure to be erected on the pier. January weather on England's south coast can be cold and/or wet, so a completely outdoor ceremony would have been problematic. However, it must be said that one recurring phenomenon gracing appearances by Her Majesty is a mystifying meteorological effect described by the British press and public alike as "Queen's weather." And although it was certainly not balmy, Queen's weather prevailed yet again that historic afternoon. It had poured rain when first *Queen Mary* had been launched in Scotland back in 1934.

The only large permanent structure on the dock peninsular is the Queen Elizabeth II terminal, used for embarking and disembarking passengers. As its bulk would have screened much of the vessel from sight, it remains an inadequate venue for naming a ship. Southampton's traditional christening place is just to the north, an unobstructed, open-air area identified as the Test Quay, named after the river that flows past it to sea. These days, much of the Test Quay serves as a giant parking lot for vehicles transshipping through the port. Well before the January ceremony, dozens of road-scrapers, cars, and trucks had to be relocated.

In their place was erected a completely enclosed auditorium with an ingenious breakaway wall facing the water. Accommodated within would be the launch party, the band of the Royal Marines, the Royal Philharmonic orchestra, soloists, a choir, and seating for two thousand guests.

On her final Southampton entry before the christening, inbound *QM2* did not turn about ready for departure as usual but remained facing upriver. Two overhead gangways had been used to facilitate embarkation for overnight visitors; one of them was new, because ironically, those used normally for smaller *Queen Elizabeth 2* were positioned too far apart for *Queen Mary 2!* Once her overnight passengers had disembarked, the vessel was inched northward, remaining connected to the terminal by one overhead gangway but in prime position along the Test Quay, bows aligned in front of the newly built auditorium.

By my count, *QM2* is the eighteenth ship and sixth passenger vessel Her Majesty has christened over her more than half-century reign. As Princess Elizabeth, Her Royal Highness named Cunarder *Caronia* in 1948. In the mid-fifties, Her Majesty christened *Southern Cross*—the first vessel with a funnel at the stern—and the second *Empress of Britain*. In 1967, she named *Queen Elizabeth 2,* not, as is often thought, after herself but as the second ship named *Queen Elizabeth;* hence, the vessel's correct Arabic numeral as opposed to the patently incorrect Roman numeral. Then in 1995, the queen christened *Peninsula* and Orient's *Oriana*.

Before *QM2's* christening bottle—a jeroboam of Veuve Clicquot—was encased in its protective netting; its glass sides were carefully scored with a file to ensure efficient breakage. Understandably, Emily Mathieson was adamant on that point: "The bottle must break!"

Prior to the ceremony, the band of the Royal Marines played a medley, including "Rule Britannia," "Anchors Aweigh," and concluding with Elgar's "Pomp and Circumstance." Then, at 4:05 P.M., everyone rose to their feet as the christening party entered: Her Majesty, Prince Philip, Micky Arison, President Conover, and newly

Above from left to right: Micky Arison, Pamela Conover, Commodore Warwick, and Her Majesty pause at the podium during the naming ceremony. *Opposite:* The Royal Choral Society and the Royal Philharmonic Orchestra perform the final movement of Beethoven's Ninth Symphony in front of the newly christened *Queen Mary 2*.

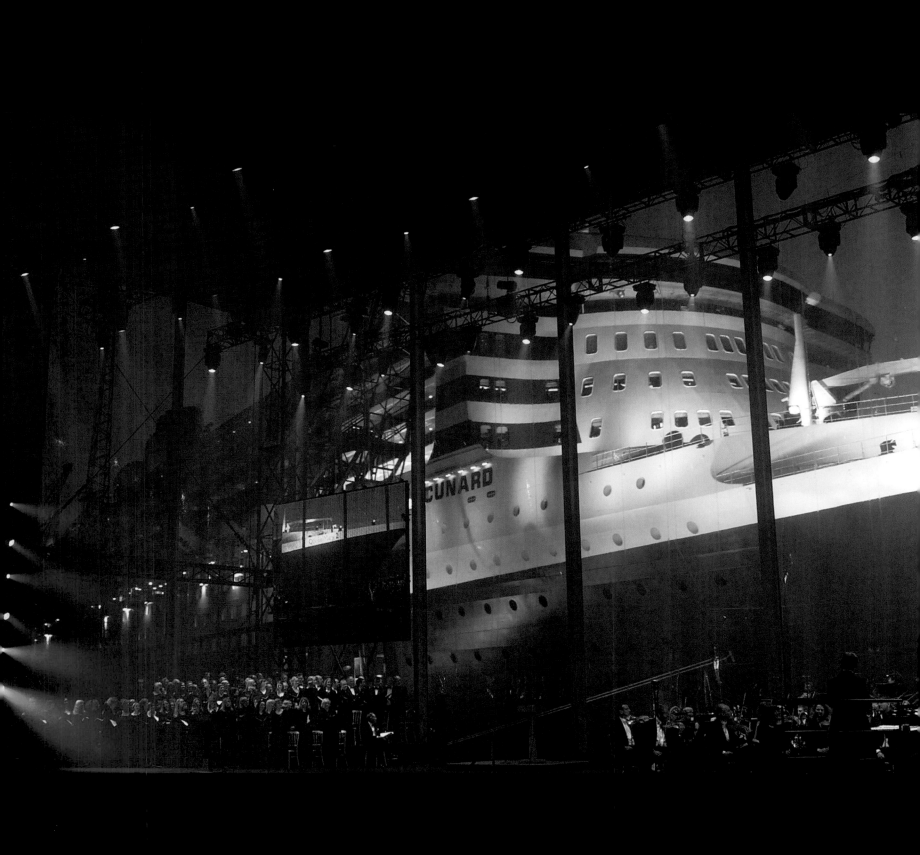

designated Commodore Ron Warwick took their places in the front row. Master of Ceremonies for the occasion was Michael Buerk, a distinguished British Broadcasting Corporation newsreader. First order of business was two verses of Britain's national anthem, "God Save the Queen," played by the Royal Philharmonic under the direction of Anthony Inglis.

First at the podium was the afternoon's main speaker, Cunard's President Pamela Conover. She spoke feelingly about her company's pride in the new ship, the significance of the occasion, and the signal honor of the royal benison about to be conferred.

Then a four-minute video—*For Queens and Country*—was projected onto twin screens, a splendid recapitulation of the company's recent history. Shown, too, was the Royal Mail's postal banner that would fly from *Queen Mary 2*'s yardarm. As a condition of that privilege, the vessel must embark a token bag of mail for delivery to the United States, perpetuating Samuel Cunard's mandate and entitling the company to use the venerable prefix RMS—Royal Mail Ship—before the vessel's name.

Then, with a stunning coup of theatrical legerdemain, the theater's seaward wall dropped abruptly to reveal the floodlit forepart of *Queen Mary 2*. Against that inspiring background, two musical selections were performed. First, pop singer Heather Small serenaded the audience with "Pride." Then Jim Motherwell, the Queen's soon-to-retire

personal piper, played atop the vessel's bow, piping "Amazing Grace." Following his haunting and evocative solo, the hymn was gloriously reprised by soprano Lesley Garrett, accompanied by the full orchestra and chorus.

The Bishop of Winchester, the Right Reverend Michael Scott-Joynt, offered his blessing for the vessel. Within the text of his benediction, he included *en francais* a moving acknowledgment of the tragic accident at St.-Nazaire two months earlier.

Then came the moment for which everyone had been waiting. To the accompaniment of a special Royal Marine fanfare composed for the occasion, Commodore Warwick requested Her Majesty's presence at the podium. After she mounted the stage, Cunard's youngest cadet, Rebecca Atkinson, presented her with a special bouquet of *Queen Mary 2* roses. Then Her Majesty intoned, for the first time, the vessel's proposed name, couched within those time-honored words that have ushered so many immortals into service, "I christen this ship *Queen Mary 2,* and may God bless all who sail in her!" After completing the sentence, she pressed the podium's button.

With a crunching pop, three liters of foaming champagne cascaded down *Queen Mary 2*'s bow plating. At the same moment, up on the bridge, officer of the watch Tim Armstrong activated a triple, booming salute from the vessel's Tyfon whistles. The crowd applauded and cheered, and the entire assemblage, from Her Majesty to Arison to

Conover to the audience and musicians and Royal Marines, beamed: a moment of unalloyed, congratulatory delight. Before the Queen resumed her seat, the Commodore called for and led three rousing cheers for Her Majesty.

Fireworks conjoined with christenings are not novel but these fireworks not only filled the sky but were also positioned on board the vessel as well as the pier beneath it. The musical accompaniment was sublime—the final movement of Beethoven's Ninth Symphony, Schiller's "Ode to Joy," with full chorus and orchestra, cued exquisitely to every pyrotechnic salvo. The combined music and fiery spectacle was as exhilarating as it was moving, and Eric Flounders's prediction about "not a dry eye in the house" was, by later agreement, fully justified.

Queen Mary 2, named by the same sovereign who baptized her predecessor thirty-seven years earlier, had entered formally into service. There was a gala dinner on board that evening in the Britannia Restaurant and an overnight tied up alongside that gave hundreds of christening guests an unforgettable evening aboard the remarkable vessel they had just seen so splendidly named.

The next morning, christening guests disembarked, and participants for a charity benefit for Britain's The Lord's Taverners trouped on board for an overnight cruise. The ship would be back in Southampton on Saturday morning and, during that final in-port weekend, Cunard senior officers and shore staff came on board for a tour of the ship

and lunch; among them was a reunion of retired masters including Robin Woodall, Peter Jackson, Lawrence Portet, Bob Arnott, and Chief Purser Bryan Vickers.

Then it was sailing day, January 12, 2004, start of the vessel's maiden voyage to Fort Lauderdale. All afternoon, a full complement of passengers was processed through the packed lounge of the *Queen Elizabeth II* terminal, waiting patiently for their turn to embark. By 5:00 P.M., they and most of their luggage were on board. They were greeted in the Grand Lobby by a corps of welcoming, white-gloved stewards and conducted to their cabins; thoughts of unpacking were rejected in favor of impatient exploration of the new ship. Near sailing time, passengers thronged the vessel's portside railings on both the promenade decks as well as hundreds of balconies, anticipating the moment of departure. The mood on board was electric. Not merely overnight, invited guests, these jubilant shipboard tenants rejoiced in the distinction of being *Queen Mary 2*'s first true passengers.

"Queen's weather" held for the departure, cool and dry without the gales predicted by the newspapers. *Queen Mary 2* glowed like a giant steel beehive as last-minute luggage was loaded. Tugs had long since assembled offshore, and mooring lines along the pier were not singled up until 6:30 P.M. At the bow, the Blue Peter came down. More than eleven hundred feet aft, Commodore Warwick ordered the red duster to remain in place; observed via one

Opposite: Fireworks light the sky above *Queen Mary 2. Above:* A mustering of maitre-d'hotels: *(left to right)* Assistant Maitre-d'hotel Konrad Pierzchala, Senior Sommelier Olav Paulat, Assistant Maitre-d'hotel Rada Barba, Senior Maitre-d'hotel David Thompson, Assistant Maitre-d'hotel Valerie Taylor; Assistant Maitre-d'hotel Xavier Resillot.

of the bridge's closed-circuit monitors, he finds it a useful guide for monitoring the wind's direction and force.

Now he, Staff Captain Chris Wells, and the Trinity House pilot Ray Smart were huddled on the port bridge wing; the red-and-white "H" flag, the pilot's flag, flew from the yardarm. Sheltered from the evening chill by the terminal's doorway, a military band, inevitable and endearing feature of every Southampton sailing, played martial airs. As final cables were slipped and the great black wall of hull glided majestically away from the quay, the strains of "We are Sailing" came plaintively across the water.

The vessel left the pier and, very slowly, proceeded stern first upstream opposite Southampton's Town Quay, surrounded by a flotilla of packed excursion boats, yachts, and small craft, even a Red Funnel Ferry taken out of service and chartered to spectators. There, QM2 stopped for a final fireworks display, a pyrotechnical salute rocketing up from a barge close by the port side. After the last firework had been fired, Commodore Warwick responded with a booming farewell on his Tyfon whistles to crowds lining the shores of QM2's home port. Only then did he order the ship moved forward, initiating the maiden voyage to Florida.

There followed a twenty-four-mile, in-harbor passage, Cunard's traditional trail to sea. With a harbor launch in the van, QM2 passed through Southampton Water and entered the Solent, circumventing the dangerous shallows of the Bramble shoals with a reverse S-turn. Her course due east then south, she passed Cowes to starboard and Portsmouth to port before finally slowing by the Nab Tower.

There, Queen Mary 2 disembarked Captain Smart. As the pilot boat cleared away from the hull in a graceful arc for the voyage back upharbor, he lingered on the open deck, waving farewell to the bridge before seeking the cabin's shelter. High atop the vessel, a flutter of obligatory in-port flags were lowered—pilot flag, postal banner, company house-flag, and red ensign; at the poop railing, another red ensign was secured. On mooring decks fore and aft, crewmen completed that inescapable ritual of departure, repainting the abraded steel where hawsers deployed in port had chafed protective paint from around the fairleads. Double crew watches, mandatory in port, stood down, and master and staff captain turned the bridge over to the officer of the watch.

Gathering speed, the liner stood off into the gusty winter night, bearing gently to starboard. Fully victualed and bunkered, RMS Queen Mary 2 had shrugged off land and returned to her native element, under purposeful way at sea. The new Commodore was aboard, the entire crew in place, and the Grand Lobby awash with passengers heading for the Britannia Restaurant and the Grills. On whatever voyage the vessel would sail over decades to come, things would never be quite the same because a maiden voyage is utterly and gloriously unique.

Two idyllic sea days were in store before next landfall far to the south at Madeira. Micky Arison's vision and Stephen Payne's first line on a piece of drafting paper, initiated five years earlier, had metamorphosed into this incomparably graceful giant breasting Atlantic swells that rolled up-Channel.

Sir Samuel, doubtless absorbing the scene from his celestial vantage point, could not but approve.

Above: Bearded Commodore Ron Warwick poses with three of his most senior officers: *(left to right)* Staff Captains Chris Wells and Martin Stenzel, Commodore Warwick, and the vessel's relief master Paul Wright. *Opposite:* A reflective moment at sunset of *Queen Mary 2* during twenty-four-hours of maneuvering practice. *Overleaf:* Next to the Chart Room on Deck 3, the Veuve Clicquot Champagne Bar overlooks the atrium. (© MICHEL VERDURE)

Twenty-first Century Cunard Shipboard

Ships that pass in the night are soon forgotten but nights that pass in a ship are remembered forever.

—Anonymous

In 1967, the late Walter Lord, doyen of maritime historians, sailed eastbound as a passenger aboard *Queen Mary*. His purpose was twofold—to get to Europe and also to be on board when the two consorts passed one another for the last time, an event promoted by Cunard as "the last encounter of *Queens* on the western ocean."

Monumental changes lay over the horizon: *Mary* was already destined for retirement in Long Beach, California, and though *Elizabeth* would soldier on with the *France* for another year, she would also end up stateside, moored in Florida's Port Everglades. Their last joint crossing would, in a theatrical sense, bring down the curtain on an unforgettable run, starring two immortals that had excelled in the most successful transatlantic production of all time.

Because of the exigencies of their respective schedules, the *Queens* would meet well after dark, perhaps too late for many. Eastbound passengers are notoriously sleep-deprived by their twenty-three-hour sea days. Both masters diverted towards one another, shrinking the sixty-mile gap that normally separated the company's east- and westbound lanes. Lord's notes convey to perfection the mood on board:

25 September: During the auction pool, word spread that the staff captain had announced to the lounge that we'd pass the QE about 2:15 A.M. The pool ended around 1:30 and just before 2:00, left the smoking room to see what was going on. Loudspeaker was just announcing that QE is 15 miles away . . .

Check Promenade Deck and can see QE's lights on the horizon. . . . By now, the whole Mary is a bedlam. . . . Passengers are pouring out in evening clothes, pajamas, everything. Even the staff captain rushing about.

Loaded with cameras, (we) look out and ahead. QE much closer now. . . . We swarm to the Boat Deck rails, many with cameras in wistful hope of a picture. I have my Minox, Rollei and binoculars. Now the ships are almost abreast. We are passing very very close, and QE looks magnificent.

Their bows crossing, the two giants tore past one another, port to port. Both masters braved the slipstream out on

their respective bridge wings, caps doffed, and Tyfon whistle controls to hand. The sound of joint salutes racketed across the intervening waves, three shattering blasts overlapping and echoed by a measured but fervent response. Their vigil rewarded, passengers along both boat deck railings cheered, waved, and took photographs. As hundreds of cameras flashed, it seemed that the two Clyde-built hulls struck sparks as they raced by. Lord continues:

Within seconds, it's over, and she's slightly astern. She's going fast, and as huge crowds troop back inside, it's clear that this was a mass turnout by nearly everyone on board, comparable to the crowds on deck as we left New York.

He marveled at the brevity of the encounter, as *Queen Elizabeth*, her glittering broadside shrunk into a three-quarters afterview and her funnel lights extinguished, vanished into the night as abruptly as she had appeared. Lord's notes conclude:

Down to cabin within a few minutes. Lean out porthole but can't even see a speck of light now. She's gone that fast.

Almost before they had begun, meeting and moment had passed, surely the ultimate "ships that pass in the night." *Queen Mary* and *Queen Elizabeth*, those staunch consorts that had steamed in both peacetime tandem and wartime service for three decades, would never pass again. For Lord, definitive *Titanic* historian, it had been yet another evocative "night to remember."

Neither captain, the *Mary*'s Treasure Jones nor Geoffrey Marr in command of the *Elizabeth*, could have guessed that four decades after that midocean encounter, yet another *Mary* and *Elizabeth* would share eastbound passage from New York to Southampton. Rather than farewell, this was joyous transition. *QM2* was assuming the transatlantic mantle relinquished by *QE2*. Henceforth, the second *Mary* would thunder along Cunard's hallowed route while the second *Elizabeth* would revert to cruising out of Southampton. But once each year, she would cross, as of old, to New York for her annual circumnavigation.

Opposite: Starting her September builder's trials, *Queen Mary 2* heads purposefully out into the Bay of Biscay, grace and strength joyously conjoined.

In happy contrast to their predecessor namesakes, this *Mary* and *Elizabeth* will remeet time and again, either in their home port of Southampton, the Mediterranean, the Caribbean, or, each December, in mid-Atlantic, perhaps out of sight but reassuringly on station nevertheless.

As of this writing, it is impossible to speculate how long *Queen Elizabeth 2* will remain in service. Presumably, her world cruises might one day be co-opted by Panamax's *Queen Victoria*. But as for *Queen Mary 2*, we have Stephen Payne's cast-iron assurance that she will be with us until the mid-twenty-first century. And thanks to computer simulations long since essayed, we know that this giant new flagship can call at 95 percent of the ports used by her predecessor.

This chapter's "history" must be predicted rather than recorded. Nevertheless, it is easy to envision any number of *QM2*'s *voyages imaginaires* years from now. She will show Cunard's flag proudly throughout eastern and western hemispheres. During her maiden Caribbean foray in early 2004, she sails south to Rio de Janeiro—just as *Aquitania* did in 1938—offering her passenger-load four giddy days of festivities in that fabled South American port. En route she crosses the equator, rewarding her Carnival-bound passengers with an historic first: King Neptune—cruise director Ray Rouse carrying a cardboard trident and wearing a cotton wool beard—inducting some nervous, newcomer pollywogs hilariously into his domain.

Opposite: The entrance to Illuminations, *Queen Mary 2*'s on-board planetarium. (© MICHEL VERDURE) *Above:* The port-side corridor that gives access to the Canyon Ranch Spa Club. (© MICHEL VERDURE)

I can see *Queen Mary 2* juxtaposed against countless other cruising destinations. During summertime Mediterranean jaunts, she will berth beneath the looming Rock of Gibraltar and later tie up alongside at Mussolini's mid-thirties Neapolitan terminal. She will make a call at Venice, easing her record-breaking bulk into the *Statzioni Maritima* to permit her passengers an incomparable Venetian idyll. Over winters in the Caribbean, I can picture her anchored out off St. Thomas, tendering passengers ashore for a day's shopping and swimming, or moored alongside at Barbados, sunstruck beneath subtropical skies but cool withal. In high summer, she will shadow Norway's rugged coastline, rejoicing in unreal midnight sunlight; at that enchanted northern cruise's apogee, her passengers can marvel at the North Cape's forbidding eminence.

One unforgettable long voyage could surpass Rio's southernmost latitude of the inaugural season. Ron Warwick's great regret is that, throughout his long sea-going career, he never sailed around the Horn. Given the inability of post-Panamax *Queen Mary 2* to transit the canal, it is not inconceivable that one day, both vessel and her master might undertake that historic passage together. Not only a memorable voyage, it would also permit an encounter between the two *Queen Marys* at Long Beach; there could follow a triumphant Pacific tour, encompassing California, Hawaii, and all those exotic Far Eastern ports of call.

But unquestionably, the most endearing vision is *Queen Mary 2* in mid-Atlantic, basking in that gloriously detached limbo between continents, bound on a crossing that will end either with majestic progression up the North River to Manhattan or wending her way past Cowes inbound to Southampton and home. For it is out there, in Cunard country, that the vessel delivers her most rewarding promise. Rather than moored alongside some tempting littoral, the great liner is where she belongs, under way.

How will her human cargo behave throughout their crossing? They will do, on the one hand, exactly what their forebears did aboard nineteenth- and twentieth-century Cunarders. On the other hand, they will enjoy richer and more varied sea days, exploring and expropriating the delights of what Deborah Natansohn has described so cogently as their "feature-rich" vessel.

Share a bird's-eye view. At break of day, along serried balcony rows, white-robed passenger couples survey the sea, restorative coffee to hand. Along both sides of Deck 7, early morning walkers tramp their appointed circuits. Those laps complete, they and treadmill addicts from the gym join fellow passengers in the morning brightness of the Britannia Restaurant, where the slanting sun strikes prismatic sparks from crystal glasses. Up in the Kings Court, other early-bird passengers congregate, drawn by that irresistible sensory amalgam of coffee, bacon, and fresh bread. Up behind the bridge, master, staff captain, chief engineer, and hotel manager gather for a captain's meeting to discus the day's events.

Once crewmen have hosed down the teak, deck stewards organize daytime chair ranks. Since the weather is sunny but bracing, ready to hand are stacks of Cunard's double-weight, blue-red steamer rugs, perfect for shrouding outdoor readers and dreamers against that glaring, midocean chill.

Forward on Deck 3, Cunard ConneXions is astir as avid e-mailers scroll through overnight arrivals while others take chairs to learn some French or, kindness of an obliging Oxford don, the glories of Gothic architecture. Junior passengers corralled aft on Deck 6 are distracted with scissors, paste, and Crayola but clamor for the morning's scavenger hunt to begin.

Midmorning in the Winter Garden, passersby sip bouillon and ponder the daily quiz. Up one deck forward, the librarian helps a passenger track down an elusive biography, careful not to disturb postcard writers with bowed heads scribbling their quota. Five decks down in the casino, a solitary but determined matutinal gambler engages a promising slot.

On Deck 1, there is other play within the hushed purlieus of Kensington as bridge devotees absorb a lecture before being dealt the first of many hands of duplicate. Inveterate shoppers troll throughout Deck 3's inviting shops; one tries on a Chanel jacket, another evaluates canisters of Harrods tea, a third samples yet again a bewitching perfume, and a couple lingers wistfully over a seductive bauble in the jewelry display case.

Lunch beckons, and friends with a birthday in mind quaff a preliminary glass in the Veuve Clicquot champagne bar; they have already booked a Todd English table for full-blown celebration that evening. The Canyon Ranch SpaClub almost empties out as the midday meal approaches, save for a residue of sybarites who prolong their soporific soak in the pool.

There is a brisk preprandial cocktail trade up in the Commodore Club, every window table full as passengers enjoy the hypnotic spectacle of *Queen Mary 2*'s white prow forging effortlessly ahead. Atop the vessel, newly risen teenagers crowd the Boardwalk Café in quest of a pizza or hamburger breakfast. The retractable glass roof just forward is sealed against ocean winds, and, throughout the day, pool waters are roiled by swimmers and their ship's motion alike.

As the sun reaches its zenith, chatter in every dining room is momentarily quelled as Commodore Warwick broadcasts noontime details of the vessel's position and performance. Somewhere on board, the winner of the announced mileage pool cannot suppress a cry of delight.

During the afternoon, the pace slows perceptibly. Though siesta's siren song lures the susceptible to cabin or sheltered deck chair, dogged work continues in the gym. A feature film is scheduled in Illuminations while more erudite fare emanates from adjacent Cunard ConneXions. Tea awaits in the Winter Garden, and Queens Grill habitués,

Opposite: In the Bay of Biscay, a gathering of Spanish yachts serve as outbound escort to *Queen Mary 2.*

rug-bundled and cherishing tea tray in lap, gather peacefully on their stern aerie above the wake.

As the sun sets, it is time to dress. First sitting passengers in evening finery cross paths with second sitting shipmates relinquishing pool and deck chairs. Deck 3's bars are awash with midocean's well-dressed clientele. Some anticipate dinner with a pint in the Golden Lion, others with one of the Chart Room's icy martinis, yet others a flute of Veuve Clicquot to wash down some caviar. Down the Grand Lobby's staircase crescent, the casino is open for full-scale gaming. Black-tied dealers await a flood of evening punters, and the roulette wheel's hypnotic rotation has begun.

But before submitting to that endlessly captivating risk indulgence, every soul on board is preoccupied with the approaching dinner hour. All restaurant stewards are assembled in evening rig. In the Kings Court, wall panels and lights have been deployed into evening mode, transforming lido into bistro quartet. A sous-chef and his ingredients are ready in the Chef's Galley, where thirty-five chairs await lucky passengers for a soon-to-be-consumed cookery demonstration. On Deck 3, Britannia's tail-coated *maitre d'hotel* welcomes diners into his white-gloved domain.

Cruise Director Ray Rouse hovers everywhere, *QM2*'s master of revels. Forward in the Royal Court Theatre, dancers already made up for *Zing Went the Strings* check

Opposite: It is Christmas Eve as a group gathers around the Grand Lobby's piano to sing carols. *Above:* The Golden Lion is a relaxing retreat for televised sporting events and traditional pub food. (© Michel Verdure)

their costume changes, musicians tune up in the pit, and technicians preset that evening's light plot. In Illuminations, the projectionist has rewound every reel of his matinee screening, and the planetarium dome has been lowered into place for a celestial display. In the Queens Room, RADA's shipboard repertory company is poised for the first of two performances of a Stoppard one-act. In the interim, music prevails as the band plays for couples flocking onto the dance floor.

Throughout those evenings, familiar transatlantic magic prevails. Passengers stroll languidly from one great public room to the next, encountering old friends and making new ones, chatting and laughing, rejoicing in that special contentment engendered by civilized shipboard. Here is indeed a veritable *tableau vivant*, simulacrum of those virtual reality renderings imagined by company planners long before the vessel's keel was laid.

Some shipmates will stay up long after the shows are over, either as part of the boisterous crowd surrounding the casino's crap table or gathered for a nightcap in the G32 discotheque. A couple or two will reenter from the promenade deck, hair windblown and the man's dinner jacket protecting his companion's bare shoulders. Theirs has been an excursion in quest of a moon or at least a railside vigil, watching the white-black waves surge past, turmoil revealed by the illuminated spill from a thousand portholes. "Beyond the green baize door"

down in crew country, newly off-duty crewmen and -women gather in the Pig & Whistle for a relaxing pint and a gossip.

All will end their evenings with a cabin retreat, where curtains are drawn, lamps aglow, and covers turned down. Once in bed, there can be no better day's finale than a glance at tomorrow's program, a televised movie, or a bit of a chapter before complete Morphean surrender.

Her passengers asleep or at play, *Queen Mary 2* perseveres across a gusty Atlantic, remorseless and impervious to regret. Vigilant officers on the bridge or manning the engine control room monitor the liner's progress and systems, legatees of Sir Samuel's mid-nineteenth-century exemplars, guardians of a million passenger dreams.

Coincidentally, millions figure at both beginnings and ends of venerable Cunarders. One proud statistic promulgated at the time first *Queen Mary* was under construction cited the ten million rivets stitching her hull plates together. And conversely, when *Aquitania* was withdrawn in 1950, it was reckoned just as proudly that after thirty-six years

of service, "Old Reliable" had steamed three million nautical miles.

Millions of rivets, millions of miles—perfect maritime bookends and testament to the inherent strength and longevity of Cunard tonnage. Though Stephen Payne assures us that no rivets adorn *Queen Mary 2*'s all-welded hull, the cumulative mileage achieved by this latest flagship over her forty-year life span will easily surpass *Aquitania*'s figurative odometer.

How better to conclude, for this French-built vessel, than with a neat Gallic epigraph. Parisians appraising a newcomer's quality will murmur approvingly "*Bon chic, bon genre*" (good style, good breeding), dual attributes suggesting elegant turnout no less than flawless character.

The same seems gloriously apropos for *Queen Mary 2*— the *bon chic* of her profile and stunning interiors no less than the *bon genre* reliability of her sturdy, seagoing genes. *Bon chic, bon genre*: that gleaming patina atop reassuring steel characterizes to perfection this grandest ocean liner of all time.

Above: Down in the vessel's engine control room, the spotless domain of Chief Engineer Brian Wattling and Staff Engineer Neil Carney. *Opposite:* Complete with her *trompe-l'oeil*-painted forward deck crossovers, *Queen Mary 2* heads out to sea. *Overleaf:* Robert Lloyd's specially commissioned portrait of *Queen Mary 2* shows her in company with three immortal predecessors, *Elizabeth* on the left, *QE2* and the first *Mary* on the right.

Bibliography

Archer, W. J. *Cruising in the Mediterranean*. London: Jarrolds Limited. 1935

Bailey, Chris Howard. *Down the Burma Road*. Southampton: Oral History Team Southampton Local Studies Section. n.d.

Blake, George. *Queen Mary: A Record in Pictures—1930-1936*. London: B. T. Batsford Ltd. n.d.

Brinnin, John Malcolm and Kenneth Gaulin. *Transatlantiques*. Paris: Editions Robert Laffont. 1989

Brooks, Clive. *Atlantic Queens*. Sparkford: Haynes Publishing Group. 1989

Dodman, Frank. *Ships of the Cunard Line*. London: Adlard Coles Ltd. 1955

De Kerbrech, Richard P. and David Williams. *Cunard White Star Liners of the 1930's*. London: Conway Maritime Press. 1988

Diggle, Captain E. G. *The Romance of a Modern Liner*. London: Sampson Low, Marston & Co., Ltd. 1930

Ellery, David. *RMS Queen Mary*. Dorset: Waterfront Publications. 1994

Hughes, Tom. *The Blue Riband of the Atlantic*. New York: Charles Scribner's Sons. 1973

Hutchings, David F. *Caronia: Legacy of A Pretty Sister*. Market Drayton: Shipping Books Press. 2000

Kaasmann, Herb. *Oregon: Greyhound of the Atlantic*. Clark: Commercial Graphics, Inc. 1993

Lacey, Robert. *The Queens of the North Atlantic*. New York: Stein and Day. 1976

Maxtone-Graham John. *Crossing & Cruising*. New York: Charles Scribner's Sons. 1992

—*Cunard, 150 Glorious Years*. London: David & Charles. 1989

—*The Only Way to Cross*. New York: Macmillan. 1972

—*Tribute to a Queen*. Lausanne: Berlitz Publications. 1987

McCutcheon, Janette. *RMS Queen Elizabeth*. Stroud: Tempus Publishing Limited. 2001

Miller, William H. *Famous Ocean Liners*. Wellingborough: Patrick Stephens. 1987

—and Luis Miguel Correia. *RMS Queen Elizabeth 2 of 1969*. Lisbon: Liner Books. 1999

Potter, Neil and Jack Frost. *The Mary*. London: George G. Harrrap & Co Ltd. 1969

—*The Elizabeth*. London: George G. Harrap & Co. Ltd. 1965

—*Queen Elizabeth 2*. London: George G. Harrap & Co. Ltd. 1969

Prior, Rupert. *Ocean Liners*. London: Tiger Books International. 1993

Smith, Ken. *Mauretania: Pride of the Tyne*. Newcastle: Swan Hunter (Tyneside) Ltd. 1997

Spratt, H. Philip. *Transatlantic Paddle Steamers*. Glasgow: Brown, Son & Ferguson, Limited. 1951

Stevens, Leonard A. *The Elizabeth: Passage of a Queen*. New York: Alfred A. Knopf. 1968

Steel, James. *Queen Mary*. London: Phaidon. 1995

Tyler, David Budlong. *Steam Conquers the Atlantic*. New York: D. Appleton-Century Company. 1939

Warwick, Captain Ronald W. *QE2*. New York: W. W. Norton. 1993

Watt, D.S. and Raymond Birt. *The Queen Elizabeth*. London: Winchester Publications. 1947

Williams, David L. *Glory Days: Cunard*. Hersham: Ian Allan Publishing. 1998

—*Southampton*. Runnymede. Ian Allan Ltd. 1984

Winter, C. R. *The Queen Mary*. New York: W. W. Norton. 1996

Photographing an Icon

I walk the half finished Colossus, hear the crash, whang and clang of raw steel hammered, jammed and wrenched into the hull, the hiss and fiery crackle of hundreds of welders. Deck atop deck, every red or grey steel wall bears chalk scribbles, hieroglyphs for the thousands of hard-hatted workmen to read and interpret. Rough steel staircases march on an on into the sky. Vast enclosed spaces bear a chaos of tubes, wires, pipes, and silver-colored boxes strewn about in seemingly random fashion.

Dusk: I stand on a stone ledge. Below me, a shining bulbous bow large enough to house an aquarium squats attached beneath the unfinished prow. It seems an eye beneath the waves, a blunt tool to cut the wake of white waters and smooth QM2's passage. A grey and infinite illusion, the vast steel hull and superstructure stretch endlessly towards a bleak white sun. Beyond, twin pyramids of a slender high bridge gleam through a pale curtain of early morning mist.

That was the beginning. The bow designed to smooth her passage will vanish beneath the sea, to reappear like a dolphin now and then as *QM2* plows the waves. After twenty years of photographing ocean liners and cruise ships around the world, I feel as one who has caught the golden ring. Could I have been at the birth of the Great Pyramid at Giza or watched the Empire State Building rise, I would have felt the same tingling exuberance. In making this book, I have been privileged to watch and photograph the implementation and construction of a modern marvel.

QM2 is unrivalled in size, cost and luxury. What seduces me are her graceful lines, for a ship is a woman and you must fall in love with her to capture her beauty. Like ballet dancer Suzanne Farrell on point making lovely arabesques in the air, *QM2* will shed her grace on the seven seas. In Shakespeare's words from *Cleopatra*, "She makes hungry where most she satisfies." A great ocean liner becomes a legend in her time. *QM2*, I wish you fair winds on the sea roads of history.

Technical Information: My photographs were made with Canon EOS1n film cameras, and EOS1D and EOS1Ds digital cameras.

Harvey Lloyd
www.harveylloyd.com

Acknowledgments

I am indebted to a host of people, foremost among them my publisher Ross Eberman, whose patience, determination, and ingenuity inspire profound gratitude. I must also thank Harvey Lloyd for his extraordinary photographs, and my dear wife Mary for both her wisdom and support.

Other names follow, listed alphabetically and, I trust, completely: Micky Arison, Patrick Boissier, Edie Bornstein, Daniel Boulud, Barbara Broekman, Louis-Philippe Capelle, Stephen Card, Jill Cohen, Andy Collier, Pamela Conover, Julie Davis, Gerry Ellis, Todd English, Joe Farcus, Eric Flounders, Tim Frew, Jeff Frier, Michael Gallagher, Tim Gallagher, Jean-Jacques Gatepaille, David Gevanthor, Joanna Goebel, Milton Gonzalez, John Grace, Yves Guillotin, Rob Hall, Bill Havens, Martin Hegarty, Erik Hermida, Jacqui Hodgson, Kathy Howard, Isabelle Huyghe, Brenton Jenkins, Fredrik Johansson, Ellis Jones, Philippe Kasse, Bård Kolltveit, Soren Krogsgaard, Kirsten Leonard, Eric Lewis, Martin Lilly, Richard Lloyd, Robert Lloyd, Emily Mathieson, John McGirl, Chantal Mooiman, Karl Muhlberger, Sture Myrmell, Deborah Natansohn, Dick Owsiany, Stephen Payne, James Rae, Captain William Range, Larry Rapp, Robert Reynolds, Ray Rouse, Michael Sand, Linda Schultes, Captain Raymond Smart, Martin Stenzel, Frank Symeou, Mary Thomas, Robert & Tomas Tillberg, Jean Vance-Andrews, Jean-Remy Villageois, Commodore Ron Warwick, Maureen Watry, Rosemary Watt, Brian Wattling, Chris Wells, Barry Winiker, Karl Winkler, Captain Paul Wright, and Letha Wulf.

If any have been inadvertently omitted, my deepest apologies.

John Maxtone-Graham

Editors: Kirsten Leonard, Tim Frew, Jean Andrews
Production Coordinator: Joanna Goebel
Production Manager: Richard L. Owsiany

Photo Credits

The publisher extends its appreciation to photographer Harvey Lloyd and to everyone else who helped to make this book possible, in particular to Michel Verdure and Yves Guillotin / Chantiers de l'Atlantique. Special thanks also to John Maxtone-Graham and Maureen Watry / The University of Liverpool for the historical images; and to Rob Hall & The Open Agency, Three Blind Mice, and Cunard Line. Several others provided remarkable images, and all contributors are listed below.

© Harvey Lloyd
Pages 10–11, 20, 21, 23 (right), 24 (left), 25, 27, 28 (right), 29, 30, 40, 43, 44–45, 46, 57, 60, 62, 71, 72–73, 74, 76–77, 78, 80, 125, 126, 133, 134, 142–143, 144, 152, 153, 156, 159 (top and bottom; paintings by Gordon Bauwens), 160, 161, 162, 163, 164, 166, 167, 168–169, 170, 171, 172, 173, 174, 175, 177 (left and right), 178 (top and bottom) 179, 180, 185, 186, 187, 195, 196, 198 (left and right), 199, 207, and front cover.

© Michael Verdure
Pages 50, 55, 56, 58, 59, 63, 64, 65, 67, 70, 75, 79, 155, 188–189, 192, 193, and 197.

Courtesy of Chantiers de l'Atlantique
Pages 8–9, 12–13, 15, 22, 26, 33, 37, 38, 41, 42, 47, 54, 68, 127, 128, 132, 135, 136–137, 138, 141, 145, 146, 148–149, 151, 176, and 191.

Courtesy of Author's Collection
Pages 19, 31, 32 (top), 89, 90, 92, 94, 95, 96, 100, 103, 104–105, 106, 107, 112, 113, 115, 116 (left, center and right), 117, 118 (left), 119, 121, 123 (right), 130, 131, 147, and 200–201 (painting by Robert Lloyd, by permission of John Maxtone-Graham).

Courtesy of Cunard Line
Pages 4–5, 7, 16, 48, 49, 61, 81–88 (gatefold), 91, and 165 (left and right); page 69 (photo by Doug Castenado); pages 181, 182, 183, and 184 (photos by Simon Wright).

Courtesy of the University of Liverpool Library
Pages 28 (left), 36, 97, 98, 99, 101 (right), 102, 109 (top & bottom), 111, 122, and 123 (left).

© Louis-Philippe Capelle
Pages 34, 53, 129, and 154.

© John Grace
Pages 35 and 39.

Courtesy of William Archibald
Page 124.

Courtesy of Art & Enterprise
Page 190.

Courtesy of Henk Brandwijk
Page 158.

Courtesy of Carnival Corporation
Page 23 (left).

Courtesy of Ross Eberman
Page 118 (right).

Courtesy of Maurizio Eliseo
Page 24 (right).

Courtesy of English Heritage NMR
Page 108.

Courtesy of Mary Evans Picture Library
Page 101 (left).

Courtesy of MARIN
Page 32 (bottom).

Courtesy of the Queen Elizabeth/ Seawise University Historical Collection
Page 114.

Courtesy of R.M.S. Queen Mary Foundation
Pages 120 and 150.

Courtesy of Tillberg Design
Page 52.

Courtesy of TWBA/Chiat Day
Page 51 (photo by Larry Fink)

Index

Abraham Cunard & Sons, 90
Acadia, 92, 93
accidents, 27, 39, 93, 178
Adriatic, 96
Adventurer, 69
air conditioning, 134, *135*
Alstom Chantiers de l'Atlantique, 20, 40, 126
aluminum, disadvantages of, 28, 31
America, 126
Andes, 69, 96
Aquitania, 19, 111, 158; first voyage, 110; fitting out, *109;* garden lounges, 65; mileage, 198; propellers, 35; Rio route, 120, 193
Arctic, 94
Arison, Lynn, *131*
Arison, Micky, *23, 131;* at christening, 182; on design, 20, 27; on flagship, 24; interior design, 52; on *Queen Mary 2,* 7; transfer of ownership ceremony, 178
Arison, Ted, 23
Armstrong, Tim, 184
Arnott, Bob, 185
artwork on *Queen Mary 2,* 62, 154–58
Atkinson, Rebecca, 184
Atlantic, 94
Atlantic crossings, 27, 116
Atlantic Room, 69
atriums, 62

balconies, 31, 39–40
Balmoral suite, 40
Baltic, 94
Barter, David, 126
bathing in sea water, 100, 120
Belgravia lounge, 57
Belinda King Presents, 162
Berengaria (Imperator), 19, 112
berths, 98
bloc assembly, 129
block form general arrangements, 48, 53
Blue Ribband, 20, 35, 92, 96, 102, 109
Board Room, 66
Boardwalk Cafe, 66
Boissier, Isabelle, *131*
Boissier, Patrick, 130, *131,* 140, 178
Bornstein, Edie, 52
Boston Cup, *92*
Boulud, Daniel, 52, 162, *165*
bow sections: *Queen Elizabeth 2, 32; Queen Mary 2, 10–11, 32, 33, 42,* 80
Brandwijk, Henk, 158
Bremen, 97, 109, 112
bridge section, *38,* 69, 72, 97
Britannia, 19, 91, 158; Boston and, 94; completed, 92; displacement, 96; life aboard, 57, 98, 100; maiden voyage, 7, *90,* 93, 131; *Queen Mary 2* and, 24
Britannia Restaurant, *50, 55, 56, 156;* design, 52, 54; tapestry design, 157; touring, 57, 58
British & North American Royal Mail Steam Packet Company, 92
British Carvery, 66
Broekman, Barbara, 51, *156,* 157
Buckingham apartment, 153
Buerk, Michael, 184
builder's trials, *175, 191*
Burns, George, 92, 96

cabins: 19th century, 98–100; categories, 153–54; construction, 135, 193; designing, 31; *Lusitania,* 109; mockups, 154; suites, 69; touring, 62
Cairnie, Ian, *53,* 65, 157
Caledonia, 92
Campania, 19, 101; in Cunard line, 110; *Kaiser Wilhelm* and, 102; life aboard, 98, 100; as paired ship, 115; shelter decks, 101; skylight, *99;* speed, 97
Canyon Ranch Spa Club, 54, *64,* 65
Cape Horn, 193
Card, Stephen, 158
Carmania, 7, 19, 69, 102
Carnival line, 20, 23
Caronia (Pretty Sister), 19, 102, 158
Caronia (Vistafjord), 20, 53, 120, *124,* 174, 182
Carpathia, 102, 120, 158
chamberpots, 98
Chambers, David, 174
Chart Room, 58
Cheadle, Robert, 174
Chef's Gallery, 66
Chelsea lounge, 57
children's areas, 62, 65
chillers, 134, *135*
China, 96
christening *Queen Mary 2,* 181–85
Churchill, Sir Winston, *116*
Cigar Lounge, 66
classes: designing for, 28; *Lusitania,* 106, 109; *Queen Elizabeth 2,* 124; *Queen Mary 2,* 66
classrooms, 62
Collier, Andy, *53*
Collins, Edward Knight, 94
Collins line, 94–96
Columbia, 92, 93
Columbia restaurant, 124, 157
Commodore Club, 54, 66, *68, 70,* 158
ConneXions, 52, *60, 61,* 62
Conover, Pamela, *130, 131, 181, 182;* biography, 48, 51; at christening, 182, 184; transfer of ownership ceremony, 178
Constanzi stern, *29,* 35
Conte di Savoia, 112
Costa Atlantica, 177
costs in design, 27–28
Countess, 7, 69
crew quarters, 54, 57
cruise ships compared to liners, 23
Cunard, Abraham, 90
Cunard, Edward, 96
Cunard, Henry, 90
Cunard, Joseph, 90
Cunard, Sir Samuel, *90,* 90–93, 96
Cunard, William, 94, 96
Cunard Academy, 62
Cunard line, *19,* 158; 19th-century daily life, 98–101; 20th-century daily life, 120–25; 21st-century daily life, 194–98; accidents, 93; administration, 48–52; Boston Cup, *92;* Carnival purchase, 20; challenges to, 102; cruising ships, 120; history of, 18, 90–97; piers, *95,* 109; *Queen* class, 112–18; rampant lion, *17;* sesquicentennial, 70; superliners, 102; White Star merger, 112

Dallinga, Reint, *36*
Davis, Arthur Joseph, 110
decks, 54–69, *gatefold*
designteam, 52, 53–54
Destiny class, 24, 40
Deutschland, 102
dining areas and bars: 19th century, 98–100; 20th century, *121; Aquitania,* 110; *Queen Elizabeth 2,* 124; *Queen Mary 2,* 58–61, 65–66; stewards, 165
Duncan, Robert, 92
Dynasty, 7, 69

electricity, 97, 100
elevators, 39, 66, 71
Elizabeth II, 70, *112,* 166, 182, *183,* 184
Ellis, Gerry, 126, *129*
embarkation lounges, 57
Empire Casino, 57, 157, *170*
Empress of Britain, 182
Empress of Canada (Mardi Gras), 23
engines and power: mermaid pods, 144–50, *145, 146, 147; Queen Elizabeth,* 118; *Queen Mary 2,* 35–36, 134, *134;* turbines, 102
English, Todd, 52, 54, 66, 162–65, *165*
Etruria, 97, 101
Eugenica C, 35
Europa, 112

Fantasy class, 24
Farcus, Joe, 61
fiddles, 98, 100
final speed runs, 177
fitting-out piers, *141,* 150
Fitzgerald, F. Scott, 120
float-offs and float-outs, *132,* 133, 140, *141*
Flounders, Eric, 182
Foster, Tom, 161
France, 20, 35, 129, 190
Franconia, 120
French Line, 97
funnels, 32, 36, *39,* 118, 140, 150

G32 disco, 62, *63*
G32 hull, *46, 136;* designation, 126; first cut, 130; float-offs and float-outs, *132,* 133, 140, *141;* moving, 140
GA (general arrangements), 48, 53
Gallagher, Michael, 182
galleries, 110
galleys, 57
gangway tragedy, 178
garden lounges and lidos, 65, 110, 123
Gardner, James, 116
Garrett, Lesley, 184
Georgic, 158
ghost decks, 54, 57, 62, 65
Gibbs, William Francis, 126
Gillian, Simon, 126, 166
Golden Lion pub, 57
Gonzales, Milton, 52
Grand Lobby, 54, *55,* 57, 61, 62, 154
Grant, Cary, *116*
Great Eastern, 106
Great Western Steamship Company, 96
"Green Goddess," 120

Hamburg American Line, 97, 102
HAPAG-Lloyd line, 109, 112
Hermida, Erik, *53*
Hibernia, 92, 93, 94

Hodgson, Jacqui, 174
Holiday class, 24
Holyrood apartment, 153
Hopkins, John, 177
hulls, 27, 96, 126. *See also* G32 hull

Ile de France, 20
Illuminations, 54, *60,* 61,*192*
Images photography, 62
immigration, 112
Imperator. See Berengaria (Imperator)
Inglis, Anthony, 184
interior design: Collins line, 94; *Lusitania,* 102; *Queen Elizabeth,* 116; *Queen Elizabeth 2,* 118; *Queen Mary 2,* 52–54, 116
Island Venture, 53

Jackson, Peter, 185
Johanssen, Fredrik, 48, 53
Jones, Ellis, 161
Jones, Treasure, *120, 190*

Kaiser Wilhelm der Grosse, 102, *103,* 106
keel laying, 130
Kensington lounge, 57
King, Belinda, 162
King's Court, 65
Kipling, Rudyard, 106
Kitching, Colin, 174
Knightsbridge lounge, 57
Korkoid linoleum, 120
Kungsholm, 53
Kvaerner Masa, 27, 129

La Piazza, 66
Laconia, 120
Lamour, Dorothy, *116*
lavatories, 98
Legend of the Seas, 129
Leigh-Bennet, E. P., 112
Lennon, Dennis, 118
Leviathan, 126
libraries, 66
lidos, 65
lifeboats, *30, 74*
Lilly, Martin, 161–62
liners, 20; 19th-century daily life, 98–101; 20th-century daily life, 120–25; 21st-century daily life, 194–98; air flight and, 116
Lloyd, Robert, 198, *200*
Lookout, 66
Lord, Walter, 174, 190
Lord's Taverners, 185
Lotus restaurant, 66
Louis Seize restaurant, 110
Lucania, 94, 101
Lusitania, 19, 104, 107, 158; design, 102, 110; dining areas, 58, 110; life aboard, 106–9; maiden voyage, *103–4,* 109; as paired ship, 115; propellers, 35; sinking, 106; turbines, 102

mail ships, 90, 92, 94, 110
Mardi Gras (Empress of Canada), 23
Margaret, 90
MARIN (Marine Research Institute), 32
Maritime Quest, 54
Marr, Geoffrey, 190
Mathieson, Emily, 182

Mauretania and Mauretania II, 19, 107; design, 102, 110, 112; dining areas, *58,* 110; hull paint, 120; Kipling on, 106; models of, 158; as paired ship, 115; preservation of, 110; propellers, 35; smoking room, *108;* speed, 109
McGirl, John, 165
McIver, David, 92, 94
McKay, Alex, 101
McKenna, John, 154
mermaid pods: design of, 35, 144–50; illustrations, *15, 34, 35, 145, 146, 147*
Michelangelo, 27, 39
Millar, James, 102
Millennium class, 53
Minnows pool, 65
models, 32, 158
Moore, Richard, 27
Motherwell, Jim, 184
Mouzourides, Eric, 53, 54
Muhlberger, Karl, 165–66, 174

Nancy, 90
Napier, Robert, 92
Natansohn, Deborah, 51, 144, 161, 194
newbuildings, 18
Nieuw Amsterdam, 35
noise, 98
Normandie, 20, 35, 39, 112
North German Lloyd line, 102, *103*
Norway class, 20
nursery and playrooms, 62

Ocean Books, 66
Oceanic, 35
Olympic, 158
orchestras, 120, 162
Oriana, 182
owner's trials, 177
Oxford University, 52, 62

Pacific, 94, 96
paddle wheelers, 90–93, 96, 98
painting hull, 140
Panama Canal, 20
Panamax, 31
Paris, 20
Parsons, Sir Charles, 102, 106
Payne, Stephen, *24, 129;* on air draft, 20; balconies, 39–40; block form GA, 48; on bridge, 69; design research, 20–27, 36–39; at endurance runs, 177; engine sizing, 134; at float-out, 140; on interior design, 48; on *Queen* class, 118; on sea trials, 166; "Stephen's pocket battleship," 126; transfer of ownership ceremony, 178
Peninsula, 182
Pennsylvania, 97
penthouse cabins, 154, *155*
Persia, 19, 96
Peskette, Leonard, 110
Peto, Harold, 102, 108
Philip, Duke of Edinburgh, 70, 166, 182
piers, *95,* 109, *141,* 150
Pig & Whistle, 57
pilots, 31, 186
Pimental, Larry, 51, 62, 69, 70
pitching, 32
planing surfaces, 32
Plewka, Schmidt, Ulla, 157
pods. *See* mermaid pods

pools: *Aquitania,* 110; *Caronia,* 124; *Queen Mary,* 123; *Queen Mary 2, 64, 64,* 65, 66, *79*
Porter, Lawrence, 185
prefabricated construction, 27, 130
Pretty Sisters, 102, 110
Princess, 7, 69, 70
Princess Grill, *58,* 66, 124
promenade decks, 65, 101, 123
promenades, 28
"pronking," 158
propellers: adoption of, 96, 97; *Queen Mary 2,* 35, *145, 146, 147*
Purser's Desk, 57

Queen Anne suite, 69
Queen Elizabeth II, *181, 182*
Queen Elizabeth, 19, 24, 114, 115, 118, 158, 198, *200;* construction, *36;* fire, 24, 116; loyalty to, 115; maiden voyage, 112; midocean meetings, 190; as paired ship, 115; sports deck, *89;* wartime role, 112, 115
Queen Elizabeth 2, 19, 119, 158, 198, *200;* bow, *32;* Captain Warwick and, 7, 70; design, 53, 116–18; dining areas, 66, 124; as last Atlantic liner, 23; life aboard, 124; menus from, 166; midocean meetings, 174, 190, 193; promenade, 28; Queen Elizabeth and, 182; ship models in, 158; staff transfers from, 174; staircases, 28; tapestries, 157; theater, 166; Tyfon whistle, 153
Queen Elizabeth suite, 69
Queen Mary, 49, 113, 115, 117, 118, 122, 123; bridge design, 39; British design of, 48; as hotel, 116; illustrations, *19,* 158, 198, *200;* life aboard, 120–24; loyalty, 115; loyalty to, 7; as paired ship, 115; passing *Queen Elizabeth,* 190; rivets, 198; speed, 96; Tyfon whistle, 150; Veranda grill, 162
Queen Mary 2: artwork, 154–58; balconies, 39–40; block form GA, 48, 53; bow, *32, 33, 42, 80, 138;* bridge, 69, 72; cabins and balconies, 31, 39, 62, 69, 135, 153–54, 193; Commodore Warwick and, 7; children's facilities, 62, 65; christening, 181–85; classrooms, 62; Constanzi stern, *29,* 35; construction, *44–45;* deck design, 54–57; deck tour, 54–69; design research, 20–27, 32, 35, 36–39; diagrams, *gatefold;* dining areas and bars, 58–61, 65–66, 162–65; economic factors, 27–28; engines and power, 35–36, 134, *134,* 140; entertainment, 161–62, 177; fitting out, 140, *141,* 150; float-offs and float-outs, *132,* 133, 140, *141;* funnel, 36, *39,* 140, 150; gangway tragedy, 178; garden lounges and lidos, 65; ghost decks, 54, 57, 62, 65; Grand Lobby and atriums, 62; hull, *46,* 126–30, *128, 136;* illustrations, *19,* 198, *200;* interior design, 52–54; as international effort, 48; keel laying, 130; life aboard, 194–98; lifeboats, *74;* maiden voyage, *12–13,* 185–86; maneuvering, 31; mermaid pods, *34,* 35, *35,* 144–50, *145, 146, 147;* midocean meetings, 174, 190, 193; models of, 32, 158; painting, 140; propellers, 35; rose, 52, 184; sea trials, 150, 166, 177–78, *191;* shipyard, 40;

shops, 61; size implications, 20, 31–32; speed, 35; stabilizers, 35, 134; staff from *Queen Elizabeth 2,* 174; staircases and elevators, 57, 58, 66, *71,* 153; steel construction, 28–31, 126–30; theaters and amphitheaters, 61; tonnage, 20; transfer of ownership ceremony, 178; Tyfon whistles, 150–53, 184; upper structure, 36–39
Queen Mary suite, 69
Queen Victoria, 53, 193
Queen Victoria suite, 69
Queens Grill, 54, *58,* 66, 124
Queens Room, 54, 58, *59,* 124
"Queen's weather," 182, 185

Radiance class, 53
rampant lion, 17
Range, Bill, 31
Rapp, Lawrence, 51–52
recreation, 66, 110, 123
refrigeration, 97, 100
Rennesland, Thomas, 165, 174, 181
Rex, 112
rolling, 32
roses, 52, 184
rotating mermaid pods, 147
Rotterdam class, 24, 27, 97, 177
Rouse, Ray, 174, 177, 193
Royal Academy of Dramatic Art, 52, 161, 166
Royal Caribbean line, 129
Royal Court Theatre, 54, 61, *161*
Royal Mail Ships, 184
Royal Navy mail officer, 94
Royal Philharmonic, 184
Royal William, 90
rudders, 35, 147

S. Cunard Company, 94
Sagafjord, 53
salons, 66
saloons, 98
Samaria, 120
Savannah, 18
scending, 32
Scheepers, Arjan, 174
Scotia, 96
Scott-Joynt, Michael, 184
sea trials, 150, 166, 177–78, *191*
Sea Venture, 53
sea water, 100, 120, 124
seasickness, 98
Seawise University, 116
Servia, 19, 97
shade decks, 101
Sharp, Guy, 165, 181
shelter decks, 101, 109
shipbuilding and shipyards, 27, 40
shops, 61
Shore Excursion Desks, 57
Sir Samuel's Wine Bar, 61
size: *Aquitania,* 110; *Lusitania,* 109; *Pretty Sisters,* 102; *Queen Mary 2,* 31–32
skegs, 35
skylights, 101
Small, Heather, 184
Smart, Ray, 186
smoking rooms, *108,* 110, 123
Song of the Machines, 106
Southern Cross, 182
Southampton, 181
speed: *Lusitania,* 109; *Queen Mary 2,* 35, 177

sponsons, 93, 98
sports decks, *89*
St.-Nazaire, 20
stabilizers, 35, 134
Stage Electrics, 162, 177
staircases: *Queen Elizabeth 2, 28; Queen Mary 2, 43,* 57, 58, 66, 153
Statendam class, 24, 27
steam engines, 93
steel construction, 28–31, 31, 126–30
"Stephen's pocket battleship," 126
stern design, 32, 35
stewards, 101, 165
suites, 69
superstructure: prefabrication, 130; *Queen Elizabeth 2,* 28, 31; *Queen Mary 2,* 36–39
Symeou, Frank, 53, 54

Tables of the World restaurant, 124
Test Quay, 182
thalassotherapy pools, *64*
theaters and amphitheaters, 61, 161, 177
Thomas, Mary, 52, 166
Tillberg, Robert, *52*
Tillberg Design, 52–53, 154
Titanic, 120
Todd English restaurant, 66, *67,* 162–65
transfer of ownership ceremony, 178
"tributes to Neptune," 98
Tung, C.Y., 116
turbines, 35–36, 102, 109, 134, 140
Turbinia, 102, *106*
Tyfon whistles, 150–53, 184

Umbria, 19, 97, *98,* 101
United States, 32, 96, 126

Vaterland, 35
Veranda grill, 112, 123, 162
Vesta, 94
Veuve Cliquot, 52, 182
Veuve Cliquot Champagne Bar, 61
Vickers, Bryan, 185
Vistafjord. See Caronia (Vistafjord)
Voyager class, 40, 53, 129

Warwick, Bil, 70
Warwick, Ron W., 7, *69, 129, 131;* biography, 69–70; on Cape Horn, 193; on Carnival purchase, 23; christening ceremony, 184; keel laying, 131; on phones on the bridge, 153; *Queen Mary 2* maiden voyage, 185; shakedown cruise, 181; speed trials, 177; transfer of ownership ceremony, 178
Washington, 97
Watt, James B., 109
Wells, Chris, *178, 186*
whistles, 150–53
White Oak, 90
White Star line, 24, 112, 158
White Star service, 165
Windsor apartment, 153
Winkler, Karl, 162, 165–66, 174
Winter Garden, 65, 157
Woodall, Robin, 185
Woodruff, Henry, 93
Wright, Paul, 70
writing rooms, 66